lonely planet

POCKET CANCÚN & THE RIVIERA MAYA

Regis St Louis & Mara Vorhees

Contents

Top: Museo Maya (p52), Cancún
Bottom: Isla Holbox (p75)

Plan Your Trip 4

Explore Cancún & the Riviera Maya 29

FROM TOP: CK-TRAVELPHOTOS/SHUTTERSTOCK; DARIOAYALA/SHUTTERSTOCK

Cancún & the Riviera Maya Toolkit 141

★ Top Experiences

The Journey Begins Here

Azure Caribbean waters and golden beaches make a spectacular backdrop for wide-ranging adventures in Cancún and the Riviera Maya. This is the place for sunrise walks along sandy shorelines, wide-eyed rambles through ancient cities and diving trips to coral reefs teeming with marine life. There are enchanting islands to explore and otherworldly cenotes, the sapphire-hued pools the Maya believed were gateways to the underworld. There's much to discover and new ways of travel, thanks to the recent completion of the much-heralded Tren Maya rail line that loops around the peninsula. – *Regis St Louis*

Regis St Louis

@regisstlouis

Regis has written extensively about Mexico and many other destinations in Latin America. He has contributed to more than 100 Lonely Planet titles.

Mara Vorhees

havetwinswilltravel.com

Mara writes about family travel around the world. She often travels with her 15-year-old twins in tow.

Cenote Cristalino (p90)

ALEXEY OBLOV/SHUTTERSTOCK

THE BEST

Food & Drink Experiences

Get ready for one-of-a-kind traditional recipes, fresh-off-the-boat seafood and an eclectic mix of global cuisine. You're also in the right place for a drink, with sunset cocktails and buzzing nightspots all along the coast.

Tuck into mouthwatering *tikin xic* (fish cooked in banana leaves) right off the beach at **Casa del Tikinxic** on Isla Mujeres. (p72)

Enjoy the garden-like ambience of Playa del Carmen's **La Cueva del Chango** while sampling classic and creative recipes. (p96; pictured above)

Tuck into lobster or king crabs while mariachis sing their hearts out in the converted mansion of **Casa Mission** in Cozumel. (p136)

Join revelers from around the globe at iconic **Coco Bongo**, a Cancún nightclub famed for its performances and massive dance parties. (p55)

Bar-hop your way along Playa del Carmen's Quinta Avenida, home to Cuban jazz joints like **La Bodeguita del Medio**. (p97; pictured above)

Party by the beach in Tulum at **Papaya Playa Project**, with DJs and live bands creating an addictive seaside soundtrack. (p115)

Right: Coco Bongo (p55), Cancún

THE BEST

Diving & Snorkeling Experiences

The Caribbean coast has a wealth of world-class dive sites, particularly off Isla Cozumel, while snorkelers can enjoy encounters with sea turtles and other marine life at spots along the eastern shores.

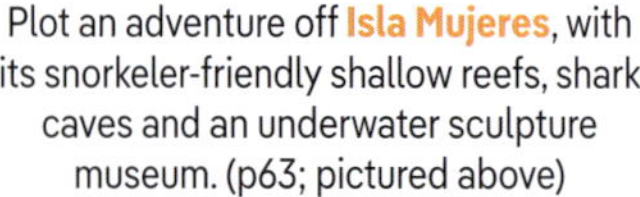

Plot an adventure off **Isla Mujeres**, with its snorkeler-friendly shallow reefs, shark caves and an underwater sculpture museum. (p63; pictured above)

Make a daytime excursion to the colorful reefs fringing **Isla Cozumel**, then return by evening for an otherworldly night dive. (p126)

Explore the passageways of **Parque Dos Ojos**, a series of spectacular cenotes comprising one of Mexico's largest underwater cave systems. (p90)

See the intersection of art and marine life while diving at **Museo Subacuático de Arte**, an artificial reef made of hundreds of unique sculptures. (p50)

Snorkel with migrating whale sharks off **Isla Holbox**, an unforgettable summer experience. (p82)

Make a trip to **Akumal** to snorkel with sea turtles, followed by a swim in a marine-rich lagoon. (p116; pictured above)

Right: Cenote Nicte Ha, Parque Dos Ojos (p90)

FROM LEFT: TRICIA DANIEL/SHUTTERSTOCK; POLLY DAWSON/SHUTTERSTOCK; MUNDOSEMFIM/SHUTTERSTOCK

THE BEST

Beach & Lagoon Experiences

Golden sands lapped by gentle surf and backed by swaying palms: this is the stuff of daydreams. Whether you want to enjoy water activities or just relax, you'll find enchanting beaches and crystal-clear lagoons.

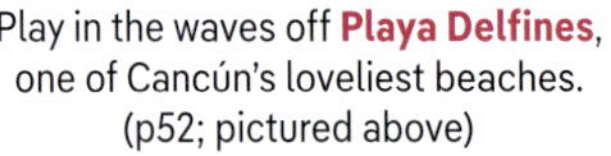

Play in the waves off **Playa Delfines**, one of Cancún's loveliest beaches. (p52; pictured above)

Watch sunrise while strolling the sands at **Punta Esmeralda**, a serene expanse of undeveloped Playa del Carmen beachfront. (p94)

Spend the day exploring the tranquil, less-visited beaches of **Isla Holbox**, returning at night to look for bioluminescence. (p75)

Sip tropical drinks while digging your heels in the sand and watching the world at play from a **beach club** in Tulum. (p114)

Take in the rich palette of blues and greens while frolicking in **Laguna Bacalar**, the Yucatán's largest lagoon. (p98; pictured above)

Rent a convertible and hit the open road in **Cozumel**, stopping at west-coast beach clubs and the wilder shores of the east. (p123)

Right: Isla Cozumel (p123)

FROM LEFT: FRANCISCO J RAMOS GALLEGO/SHUTTERSTOCK; DC_APERTURE/SHUTTERSTOCK; THEISLANDEXPLORERS.COM/SHUTTERSTOCK

WIRESTOCK CREATORS/SHUTTERSTOCK

El Castillo (p56), Chichén Itzá

THE BEST

Maya History Experiences

One of the great civilizations of the pre-industrialized world, the Maya left behind a remarkable legacy of pyramids, temples and ball courts, some dating back more than 1000 years.

Visit the mother of all Maya sites at **Chichén Itzá**, a once-grand city of striking architectural works. (p56)

Pedal your way past temples, stelae and weathered ball courts in **Cobá**, which lies amid dense forest. (p120)

Take a break from the seaside to explore **El Meco**, a Maya port that was likely active right up until the Spanish arrival. (p42)

Admire the views over the Caribbean while exploring the once-fortified Maya city of Tulum, now part of the **Parque del Jaguar**. (p106)

Visit Isla Mujeres' **Punta Sur**, once a sacred Maya pilgrimage site dedicated to Ixchel, goddess of the moon, fertility and childbirth. (p67)

Learn about the ancient human presence on the 'Island of the Swallows' at the **Museo de Cozumel**. (p132)

Best for Kids

Join local families on weekends at Cancún's **Parque de las Palapas**, with its carousel, electric kiddie cars, trampolines, street food and whimsical performers. (p34)

Take the kids on a glass-bottomed boat tour over the sculptures and artificial reef of **MUSA**, seeing mangroves and bird and marine life along the way. (p50)

Strap on a life vest and jump into **Los Rápidos**, an easy-flowing channel in Laguna Bacalar. You can also swim, rent kayaks and have a meal. (p101)

Enjoy a day at Cozumel's **Punta Sur Eco Beach Park**. Climb a lighthouse, take a boat tour, see some Maya ruins and play on the beach. (p132)

Cool off in the sparkling waters of **Cenote Cristalino**, one of the Yucatán's many natural forest-ringed swimming holes. (p90)

Best for Free

Soak in the natural pools, swim in the shallow waters and catch fine sunsets off one of Mexico's most stunning beaches, **Playa Norte** on Isla Mujeres. (p66)

Stroll the sands of **Playacar** in Playa del Carmen, seeking out the freely accessible Maya ruins just off the beach. (p94)

Take an evening walk to **Punta Coco** on Isla Holbox to see the island's best free evening show: bioluminescence sparkling in the waves. (p83)

Catch the free evening entertainment (though it's polite to tip) along Playa del Carmen's Quinta Av and **Parque Los Fundadores** – from folkloric dancers to soaring *voladores*. (p94)

Photograph stunning street art on a walk through **Cancún's Centro**, which is dotted with eye-catching works by local artists. (p40)

Perfect Days

Grab your sunglasses, swimsuit and spirit of adventure and prepare for a heady dose of Caribbean wonders, from teeming coral reefs to towering Maya ruins, then celebrate the journey over sunset drinks.

Quinta Avenida (p93), Playa del Carmen

FROM LEFT: ARKADIJ SCHELL/SHUTTERSTOCK; JASON DECAIRES TAYLOR; MIKOLAJ NIEMCZEWSKI/SHUTTERSTOCK; SECKIN OZTURK/SHUTTERSTOCK

DAY ONE

Only Have One Day?

MORNING

Start the day with a morning snorkeling trip or diving excursion at **MUSA** (p50; pictured above; sculpture by Jason deCaires Taylor), an artificial reef made from site-specific artwork and evocative sculptures. Grab a bite at **Don's Tacos & Burritos** (p54), then enjoy some beach downtime.

AFTERNOON

Get active again on a scenic (and easy-going) sunset paddling tour through the mangroves of Laguna Nichupté with **Go Kayak Cancún** (p53). With luck, you may spot dolphins, rays, crocodiles and a wide variety of bird life.

EVENING

Have dinner and drinks overlooking the lagoon at **El Fish Fritanga** (p54). If you're not ready to call it a day, head to **Coco Bongo** (p55) for late-night revelry.

DAY TWO

A Weekend Trip

MORNING

Greet the sunrise with an early morning stroll up to lovely **Punta Esmeralda** (p94) in Playa del Carmen. Grab a quick bite at **Chez Céline** (p96) and then catch the ferry to **Cozumel** (p123; pictured above).

AFTERNOON

Book a **snorkeling or diving excursion** (p126) on the colorful reefs fringing Cozumel's west coast. Look for sea turtles and other sea life, then have a late lunch and a siesta at a **beach club** (p134).

EVENING

Catch the boat back to Playa del Carmen for an evening stroll along ever lively **Quinta Avenida** (p93). Have dinner at **La Cueva del Chango** (p96), followed by drinks at **La Bodeguita del Medio** (p97).

DAY THREE

A Short Break

MORNING

Start your day in Tulum by renting a bike and pedaling out to **Parque del Jaguar** (p106) to visit impressive Maya ruins, lookout towers and lovely beaches. Take a boat trip out to the reef for some snorkeling.

AFTERNOON

Grab a quick bite in town and then head out to a cenote – those forested, turquoise-hued natural swimming holes for which the Yucatán is famed. **Cenote Azul** (p90; pictured above) is a low-key option, while bigger **Parque Dos Ojos** (p90) offers guided snorkeling excursions.

EVENING

Take a shopping stroll back in Tulum and then have dinner at **Casa Sofia** (p118), followed by the world's best mojitos at **Batey** (p115).

If You Have More Time

Before or after your time in Cancún, tack on a trip to **Isla Holbox** (p75). This offbeat island is a jumping-off point for **whale shark tours** (p82) in season. Alternatively, you can **kayak through the mangroves** (p83), get pampered at a **beach club** (p84) or wade out to sunbathe on a **sandbar** (p78). If the winds are up, you might try your hand at **kiteboarding** (p83).

By night, there are taco tours, fire shows and **live music** (p85). Or sit back at **Punta Coco** (p83), cocktail in hand, and watch the bioluminescent waves ripple across the shoreline.

After Isla Holbox, head down to **Chichén Itzá** (p56) for a look at one of the great ancient Maya cities.

From there, continue to the coast and veer south to **Bacalar** (p98), an easy-going settlement overlooking a lagoon. Head off on a boat trip, explore the old **Spanish fort** (p99) or go for a sunrise paddling excursion and then toast your travels over dinner and drinks at **La Playita** (p99) on the waterfront.

Stand-up paddleboarding, Bacalar (p98)

RUBI RODRIGUEZ MARTINEZ/SHUTTERSTOCK

A City Day Trip

A mere 30 minutes after boarding the ferry from Cancún, you'll arrive on picturesque **Isla Mujeres** (p63), with stunning beaches and a laid-back vibe. Once there, you can spend the day relaxing on the seaside – **Mayan Beach Club** (p73) on Playa Norte is a good choice. Alternatively, get active by visiting **Punta Sur** (p67; pictured above), home to a ruined temple and a scenic cliff walk. You can even get there by bike on a **scenic ride** (p68) from the ferry terminal.

In the late afternoon, head up to **Avenida Hidalgo** (p70) to stroll, snack and window-shop, followed by a memorable meal at **Lola Valentina** (p72).

On a Rainy Day

Focus your attention on Playa del Carmen's museums dedicated to **Frida Kahlo** (p95) and everyone's favorite food stuff – **chocolate** (p95). Grab lunch then take the ferry (don't worry, there are plenty of indoor seats) over to **Cozumel** (p123). From the terminal, make a mad dash (or hop in a taxi) up the three blocks to the **Museo de Cozumel** (p132; pictured above). There you can learn all about Maya history and culture as well as the island's plant and animal life in one of the region's best museums.

Finish the day with some shopping in **Los Cinco Soles** (p131), which has some outstanding handicrafts from across Mexico.

Get Prepared

BOOK AHEAD

Six months ahead
If planning to stay in a top resort during high season (December through February), make your arrangements well in advance.

One month before
Make reservations at top restaurants such as **Hartwood** (p118) in Tulum or the beachside **Casitas** (p54) in Cancún.

One week before
Reach out to tour operators and book diving excursions and other activities. Check the weather forecast.

Manners Matter

If invited to someone's home, take a small gift, such as flowers. Arrive a bit late (being on time is considered rude).

Use señor or señora/señorita, especially when requesting something.

Before dining, it's polite to receive and initiate a *buen provecho* (enjoy your meal).

When greeting or being introduced, Mexicans tend to touch: they shake hands or kiss on one cheek.

Clothing Essentials

No matter what month you come, there will be serious heat and humidity. Bring lightweight, breathable fabrics and don't forget a wide-brimmed hat.

Rain is a year-round possibility, although the biggest storms happen from June to October. Pack a lightweight rain jacket.

Pack sturdy shoes for walking around Maya ruins. Water shoes come in handy when visiting cenotes and rocky beaches.

Things to Know

Cenotes An iconic Yucatecan geological feature, cenotes (se·*no*·tays) are sinkholes formed by the corrosive effects of rainwater drilling down through porous limestone. Thousands of cenotes dot the landscape, and their crystalline waters make enchanting settings for swimming, snorkeling and sometimes diving.

Sargassum Seaweed This large brown seaweed can wash up on the beaches of the Caribbean coast year-round, but the microalgae are most prevalent from April through September. Rising sea temperatures from climate change have fueled sargassum's increased growth.

Nortes These strong 'northers' blow across the Gulf of Mexico and create gusty, cooler conditions along the coastline. They can occur from November to April and are a delight to windsurfers (but diminish visibility for divers).

TIPPING

Tipping is essential for restaurant staff, who rely on tips for their income.

Restaurants
if service is not already included

Bars
anything is appreciated

Taxis
drivers don't expect tips

Hotel staff
per day for house-keeping staff

DAILY BUDGET

BUDGET: Less than M$1200

- Dorm bed: M$300–750
- Double room in budget hotel: M$600–1200
- Street eats or economical set menu: M$40–100
- Bike rental per day: M$150–250

MIDRANGE: M$1200–2500

- Double room in comfortable hotel: M$600–1500
- Lunch or dinner in a restaurant: M$80–240
- Short taxi trip: M$35–80
- Snorkeling boat trip: M$1000–1300

TOP END: More than M$2500

- Double room in upscale hotel: from M$2200
- Dining in fine restaurant: from M$600
- Car rental including liability insurance: from M$1000 a day
- Two-tank diving trip: M$2200–2800

Currency
Mexican peso (M$)

Language
Spanish, Maya

Time
Eastern Standard Time (GMT/UTC minus five hours). Chichén Itzá is an hour behind.

TIP

At most cenotes and out on the coral reef, the use of sunscreen is prohibited (this includes so-called 'organic' or 'biologically safe' sunscreens). Instead, wear a long-sleeve rash shirt to protect against the sun.

When to Go

Cancún and the Riviera Maya are year-round destinations with inviting beach escapes and refreshing cenotes when temperatures soar, and lively festivals throughout the year.

Yucatán high season falls between December and April, when visitors from more northerly regions (USA, Europe) flood the beaches between Cancún and Tulum. These months roughly overlap with the dry season, when there are fewer showers and temperatures are lower.

The June to November rainy season brings higher temperatures, which can mean occasional downpours (but plenty of sunny skies in between). This is also hurricane season, bringing the possibility of devastating storms hitting the peninsula.

The Big Festivals & Holidays

February: The festive spirit of **Carnaval** comes alive in Cancún, Cozumel, Bacalar, Playa del Carmen and elsewhere along the coast. Catch parades, street parties and merrymaking on the days leading up to Ash Wednesday.

April: Isla Mujeres hosts **Utopia** (p146), a four-night LGBTIQ+ festival featuring top DJs from around the globe spinning in a magical island setting. Apart from joining the evening parties, you can also participate in lots of daytime activities, including yoga and wellness classes.

September: Mexico's **Independence Day** is celebrated on the evening of September 15 with late-night fireworks and revelry. Parades and street festivals happen on September 16, which is a national holiday.

Cancún Weather

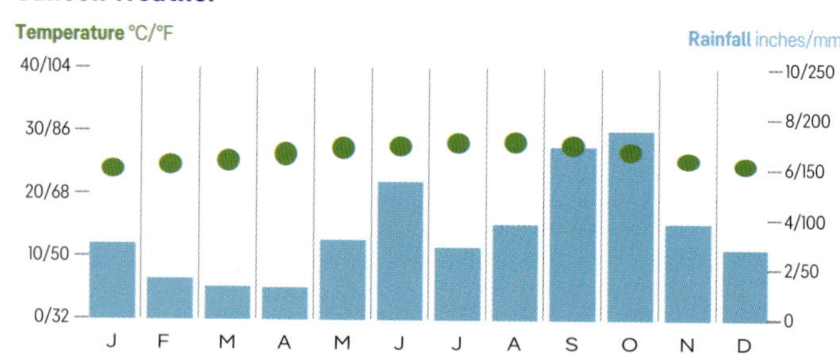

NEKOMURA/SHUTTERSTOCK

Carnaval in Cancún

November: Colorful **Día de Muertos** (Day of the Dead) altars pop up on November 1 and 2 to honor Mexican's departed loved ones.

Local Celebrations & Religious Festivals

January: Tulum stages several big gatherings this month. One of the best-known is **Day Zero**, where top DJs spin beneath a jungle-clad backdrop with laser lights and oversized art installations.

April: Isla Holbox fetes the patron saint of fishers, **San Telmo**, with a procession, food stalls and live music in the main square. The big day is April 14.

May: On Cozumel, the **Fiesta del Cedral** (p135) honors War of the Castes refugees who settled on the island in 1848. It features a time-honored Dance of the Pigs Heads.

August: In the far south, the torrid summer heat can't dampen the excitement for the **Feria Expo San Joaquín Bacalar**. The festival brings concerts, processions, amusement-park rides and plenty of eating and drinking.

ACCOMMODATION LOWDOWN

Prices are highest from mid-December to early January, when hotels can double their rates. You'll find good deals and still-decent weather during May and June and September to November. High-summer July and August offer rock-bottom prices, though increased risk of hurricanes.

Getting There

The main gateway, Cancún Airport has ATMs, money exchange, shops, cafes and car-rental agencies. A useful ADO long-distance bus station is right in the terminal.

From the Airport to Cancún & Beyond

By Taxi

Regular taxis aren't allowed to do airport pickups. If you show up without a reservation (not recommended), 'licensed' transportation services will ask for M$1500 or more to reach the Zona Hotelera. Expect to pay M$1500 to Playa del Carmen and M$2500 to Tulum – for both, taking the bus is cheaper.

By Bus

If you're staying in downtown Cancún, you can take an ADO bus *(ado.com.mx)* from the airport to the bus terminal in El Centro *(65 min, M$140)* or to the Zona Hotelera, stopping at Plaza Fiesta *(45 min, M$140)*. The airport bus terminal is also handy for reaching other destinations, with frequent departures to Playa del Carmen *(2hr, M$255)* and Tulum *(3hr, M$430)*.

By Shuttle

If you're heading to the Zona Hotelera, you can prebook a private or shared shuttle through your accommodations. You can also book through companies like Happy Shuttle Cancún or USA Transfers (aka Canada Transfers), with average prices of M$900 to M$1100.

By Train

A free shuttle connects the airport to the Tren Maya station. From there, you can ride the line south to Playa del Carmen, Tulum and Bacalar, or take the inland route toward Chichén Itzá. Ticket prices vary.

Other Points of Entry

Tulum Airport

Situated 40km southwest of Tulum, this airport has direct flights from various cities in Mexico, the USA and Canada. Regular ADO buses travel to Tulum *(45 min, M$220)* and Playa del Carmen *(1¾ hr, M$295)*. Taxis are pricey *(from M$1300 to the center of Tulum)*.

Cozumel Airport

Located 2.5km northwest of the downtown waterfront, tiny Cozumel airport has a handful of daily flights from other Mexican cities and the USA. Book a shuttle *(from M$300)* or walk 500m outside to cheaper taxis *(from M$150)*, which line up opposite Diego's Taco Stand.

Getting Around

The Yucatán has a good transport network, consisting of buses, *colectivos* and a train line (opened in 2024). There are also plenty of agencies offering car rentals. Sometimes getting from one place to another is a memorable part of the adventure, especially when hopping on ferries out to Isla Mujeres, Holbox or Cozumel.

Bus

Buses on the Yucatán Peninsula are comfortable, frequent and reasonably priced, and they link all the major towns and cities. Most destinations have one main bus terminal where all long-distance buses arrive and depart. Grupo ADO is the most prominent bus line, operating many routes around the Yucatán and beyond.

Colectivo

On much of the peninsula, vans or cars operate shared transportation services between towns and along the Caribbean coast. These vehicles usually leave when full, typically every 10 to 20 minutes. On the downside, they can get crammed and aren't ideal if you have sizable luggage. Generally, you pay when you exit.

Train

The Tren Maya, which began operating in 2024, is a 1554km railway that loops around the peninsula on several different lines: one travels from Cancún down the Caribbean coast (stopping at Playa del Carmen, Tulum and Bacalar). Another crosses the peninsula and continues south, stopping at

FROM LEFT: GEORGE WIRT/SHUTTERSTOCK; PHORTUN/SHUTTERSTOCK

ESSENTIAL APP

Download the official Tren Maya app to browse train schedules and purchase tickets.

Chichén Itzá (p56) and towns to the west. Maps and schedules are available at rutatrenmaya.com – a link on the site will take you to the ticket-purchasing site *(reservas.ventaboletostrenmaya.com.mx)*. Tickets are currently available for purchase only two weeks in advance.

Ferry

Frequent ferries connect to the region's inhabited islands. From Playa del Carmen, Ultramar and Winjet ferries depart hourly to Isla Cozumel. To reach Isla Mujeres, Ultramar ferries depart from Puerto Juárez in Cancún, while Xcaret Xailing runs from the Zona Hotelera. Ferries to Holbox are operated by Holbox Express and 9 Hermanos, both of which depart from the port at Chiquíla. For all ferries, you can purchase tickets online or at the point of departure.

Bicycle

Several towns have bicycle lanes and bike rental options, making it a good way to reach some areas. In Cancún, you can ride along the **Cancún Ciclopista** (p53), which runs for 13km between Playa Caracol and Punta Nizac. In Playa del Carmen, biking along pedestrianized **Quinta Avenida** (p93) is a great option to reach the northern beaches. Tulum has a bike path from town out to **Parque del Jaguar** (p106) as well as toward the beach, though once you reach the beach road there's no separate bike lane if you're heading into Tulum's Zona Hotelera (be careful of traffic on this narrow road). Isla Mujeres and Isla Holbox are also fine places for cycling.

Taxi & Rideshare

Taxis are widely available. Meters aren't common, so agree on a fare before getting in. Prices are quite high, especially in Cancún's Zona Hotelera and everywhere in Tulum. Uber and other rideshares are only available in Cancún (but not in the airport).

Driving in Cancún & the Riviera Maya

Getting behind the wheel can be stressful: be prepared for heavy traffic on highways, impatient drivers and parking challenges, as well as pricey rentals and fuel. On the plus side, you'll have the freedom to explore off-the-beaten-track beaches and other attractions.

Car Rentals

Before booking a car, make sure you verify the total price includes mandatory insurance. Many online rentals conveniently exclude this fee, which can add M$400 or more per day. Plan on spending around M$1000 per day for a rental, with discounts for a week or more. Be sure to inspect and photograph the car before signing the waiver and departing as security against dings and damage you didn't cause.

Road Conditions & Hazards

Major roads are generally fine, but in rural areas expect narrow lanes and bad potholes. Watch for *topes* (speed bumps), which line populated areas and sometimes appear with little notice on highways outside of small settlements. Avoid driving at night: potential hazards include unlit vehicles, rocks, pedestrians, bicycles and animals on the roads. It's always wise to take things slowly.

Fuel

Gasolina (gasoline) prices hover around M$25 per liter. Fueling stations are not self-service. Before the attendant gets underway, ensure the pump is back to zero – charging you for fuel you didn't actually receive is a common scam. Not all gas stations accept international credit and debit cards, so have pesos on hand.

TRAVEL COSTS

Train ticket from Cancún to Tulum from M$467

Ferry ticket from Playa del Carmen to Cozumel M$320

Colectivo Playa del Carmen to Tulum M$60

WALKING WISDOM

Many areas are quite walkable, including the centers of Playa del Carmen, Tulum, San Miguel de Cozumel and downtown Cancún.

DMITRY EAGLE ORLOV/SHUTTERSTOCK

DRIVING ESSENTIALS

Drive on the right.

Speed limit is generally 40km/h in populated areas, 80km/h on highways and 110km/h on toll roads.

Blood alcohol limit is 0.6g/L.

A Few Surprises

Beyond the sandy beaches and cerulean seas, Cancún and the Riviera Maya have many hidden wonders, from eye-catching street art to wildlife-rich jungles.

The Hidden Side of Chichén Itzá

Don't tell anyone, but there's a part of **Chichén Itzá** (p56) that's delightfully free from the tourist crowds. **Chichén Viejo** features 25 little-seen structures set around two plazas. The catch: it's a long walk (1.5km) from the main site. It's only open Fridays and Saturdays on guided tours *(at 9am & noon)* and limited to just 50 visitors. Go early to secure a spot; reserve when buying tickets at the main entrance.

A Little-Visited Reef

Banco Chinchorro is one of the largest coral atolls in the northern hemisphere and known for its impressive coral walls and canyons. The marine life is astonishing, with abundant coral rays, turtles, giant sponges, grouper, tangs, eels and nurse sharks. The seaside village of Mahahual (a 2¾-hour drive south of Tulum) is the gateway to the reef, with several reputable dive operators running trips, including Doctor Dive *(doctordive.com)*, Amigos del Mar *(amigosdelmar.net)* and Mar Adentro *(maradentrodiving.com)*.

Monkey Encounters & Zip-Lining

Run by a small Maya community, **Punta Laguna** (p116) is a protected reserve where visitors can enjoy some action-filled ecotourism activities. The experience starts with an incense-filled purification ceremony in hope of bringing good fortune to the day's activities. You'll then take a guided walk through the forest in search of wildlife, go canoeing and zip-lining, followed by a descent into the Cenote Calaveras – watch your step, lest you become an involuntary offering to the Maya gods.

OFFBEAT CANCÚN & THE RIVIERA MAYA

Try your hand at making *tamales* (wraps), sip Mayan chocolate drinks and watch folkloric dancing at **Pueblo de Maíz** (p135) on Cozumel.

Watch cutting-edge street art and learn about the people behind the works on an artist-led **Cancún Street Art Tour** (p42).

Catch the nightly fire and acrobatics show while sipping cocktails and dining at **Aldea Kuká** (p85) on Isla Holbox.

Dive into sparkling water in the little-known **Kapen-Ha cenote** (p114), tucked off the beach road in Tulum.

Nurse shark, Banco Chinchorro

Spider monkey, Punta Laguna (p116)

Explore Cancún & the Riviera Maya

Worth a Trip

Walking & Cycling Tours

Dive into one of the Riviera Maya's many cenotes
MARTIN CORR/SHUTTERSTOCK

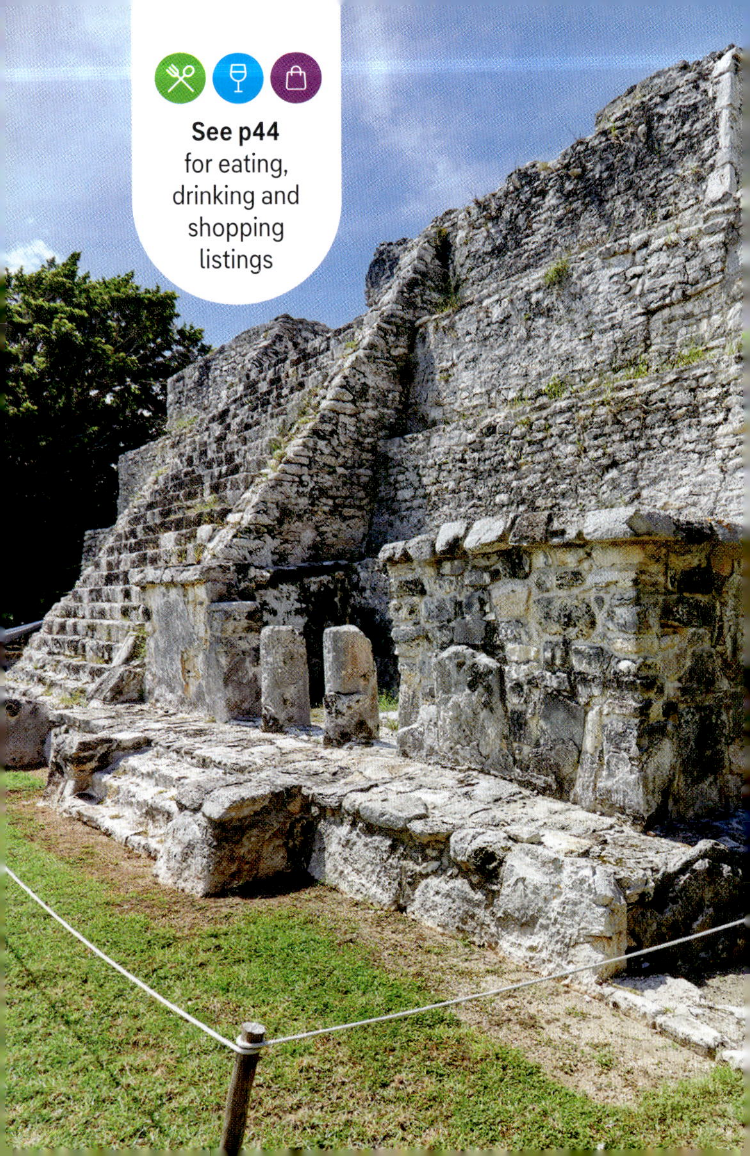

See p44
for eating,
drinking and
shopping
listings

Explore Cancún Centro

Guess what? There's a whole world outside your resort – a lively cosmopolitan city where people live, shop, work, create and congregate. Some travelers like to stay in downtown Cancún for its affordable accommodations, but in recent years it has become a destination in its own right. Spend a day in El Centro to experience contemporary urban Mexican culture, from hip-hop music to street art. Sample local restaurants and street food to get a taste of Yucatecan cuisine. And meet the Cancunenses on their own turf – in the parks, markets and streets of their hometown.

Getting Around

Bus

The main routes are R-1 and R-2, both of which connect El Centro to the Zona Hotelera. R-1 runs along Av Tulum to the ADO bus station and Puerto Juárez ferry terminal, R-2 goes to Mercado 28. R-27 heads south along Av Tulum to Plaza Las Americas. The bus fare is M$12, and the driver can usually give change.

Airport Bus

Airport buses run to/from the ADO station in El Centro *(M$140)*.

Taxi

Taxis are plentiful and affordable, as are Uber rideshares. Regular taxis are not allowed to do airport pick-ups; book a transfer in advance to avoid the overpriced services that wait at the airport.

THE BEST

MAYA SITE El Meco (p42)

DAY TRIP Isla Contoy (p36)

LATIN DANCING La Coyota Cancún (p42)

LOCAL CULTURE Parque de las Palapas (p34)

TACOS El Socio Naiz (p44)

El Meco (p42)
SAILINGSTONE TRAVEL/SHUTTERSTOCK

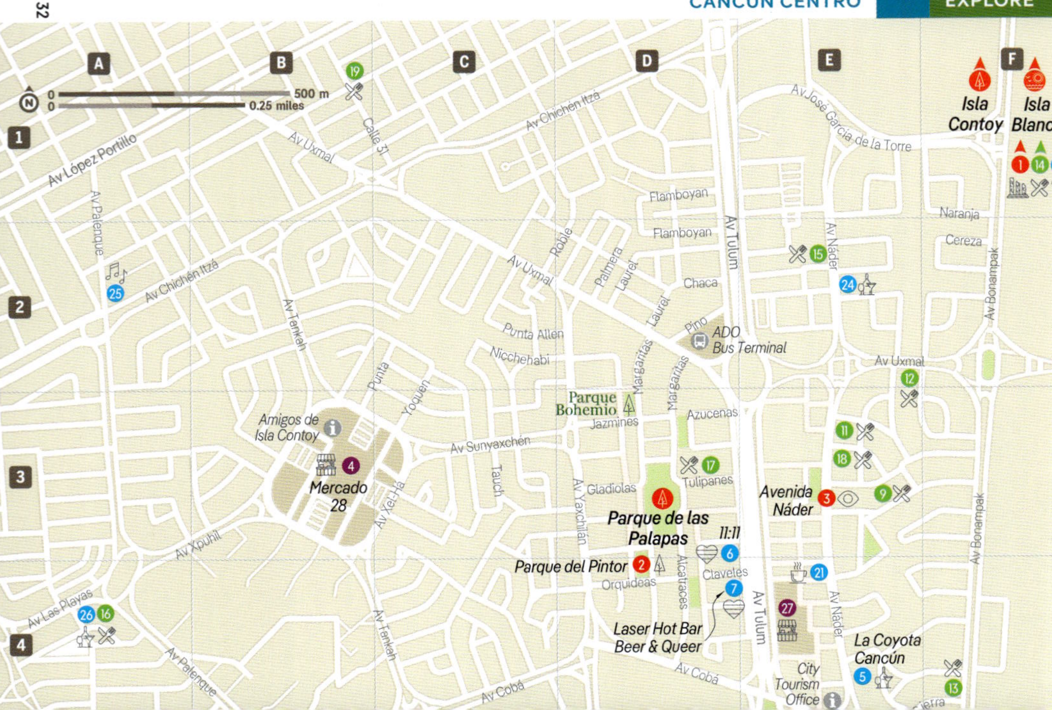
A
B
C
D
E
F
1
2
3
4
0
500 m
0
0.25 miles
Isla Contoy
Isla Blanca
1
14
22
19
Av López Portillo
Av Uxmal
Calle 31
Av Chichén Itzá
Av José García de la Torre
Flamboyan
Flamboyan
Naranja
Cereza
Av Palenque
25
Av Chichén Itzá
Av Uxmal
Roble
Palmera
Laurel
Laurel
Chaca
Av Tulum
15
Av Náder
24
Av Bonampak
Av Tenkah
Punta Allen
Nicchehabi
Pino
ADO Bus Terminal
Av Uxmal
12
Punta
Yoquen
Margaritas
Margaritas
Parque Bohemio
Jazmines
Azucenas
Amigos de Isla Contoy
4
Mercado 28
Av Sunyaxchén
Tauch
11
18
17
Tulipanes
Gladiolas
Av Yaxchilán
Av Xel-Há
Avenida Náder
3
9
Parque de las Palapas
11:11
6
Av Xpuhil
Parque del Pintor
2
Alcatraces
Claveles
Orquídeas
7
21
Av Bonampak
Av Las Playas
26
16
27
Av Tulum
Av Náder
Laser Hot Bar Beer & Queer
La Coyota Cancún
Av Tenkah
Av Palenque
Av Cobá
Av Cobá
City Tourism Office
5
13

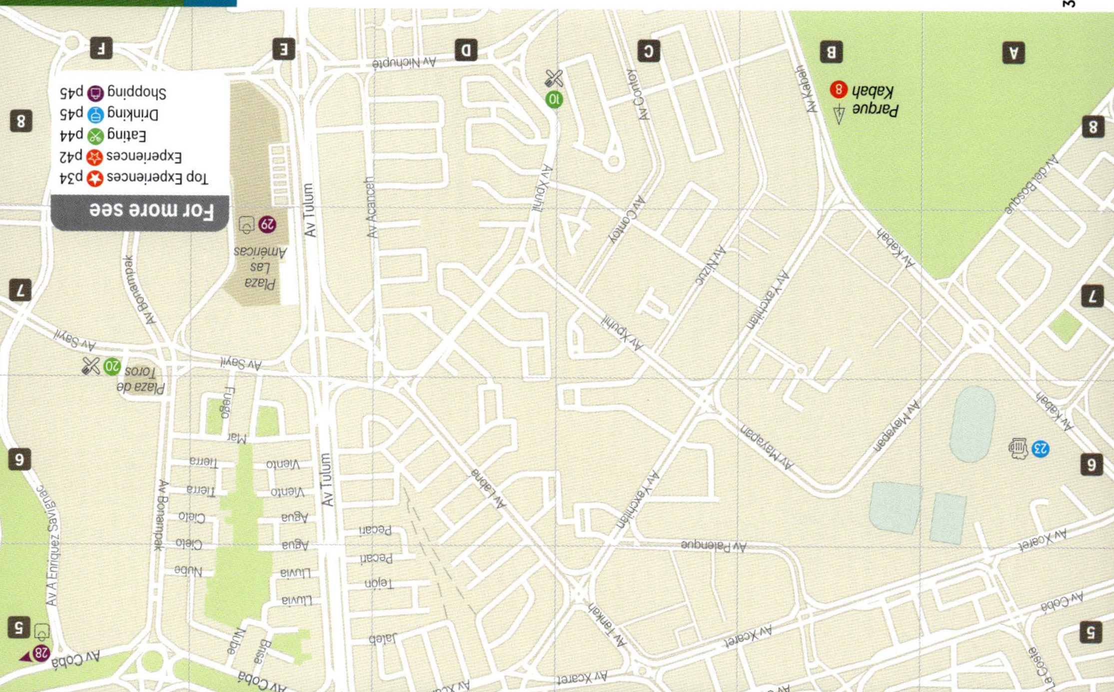
For more see
Top Experiences p34
Experiences p42
Eating p44
Drinking p45
Shopping p45
A
B
C
D
E
F
5
6
7
8
Av Tulum
Av Acanceh
Av Nichupte
Av Bonampak
Av Sayil
Plaza de Toros
Plaza Las Américas
Av Xpuhil
Av Contoy
Av Kabah
Parque Kabah
Av del Bosque
Av Nizuc
Av Yaxchilan
Av Mayapan
Av Labna
Av Palenque
Av Xcaret
Av Tankah
Av Cobá
Av La Costa
Av A Enriquez Savignac
Jaleb
Tejon
Pecari
Agua
Viento
Tierra
Cielo
Nube
Lluvia
Brisa
Mar
Fuego
8
10
20
23
28
29

★ TOP EXPERIENCE

Parque de las Palapas

Cancunenses love a good fiesta, and they make one every weekend at **Parque de las Palapas**. This city-center park springs to life in the evenings when locals come to relax with friends and family. It's a rare slice of local urban life in a city that thrives on international tourism.

MAP P32 **D3**

PLANNING TIP
People start to gather at Parque de las Palapas around 5pm, but the peak time is from 8pm to 10pm, especially on weekends.

Street Food

Parque de las Palapas is one of the city's top spots for street food (pictured), with dozens of stalls selling tacos, quesadillas and *gorditas* (corn tortilla pockets). Unique Yucatecan favorites include *panuchos* and *salbutes* (both like tacos, but with thicker tortillas), as well as decadent fried quesadillas. The permanent stalls on the park's north side are open all day, but additional food carts show up in the evening to sell traditional street desserts. Here's your chance to try the Yucatecan specialty, *marquesitas* (crispy rolled-up crepes filled with your choice of ingredients such as Nutella or Edam cheese).

Entertainment

Free live entertainment on weekends draws crowds to the park. There are often live-music and dance performances on the main stage, set under a towering *palapa* (thatched) roof. Fun for kids is nearly limitless, with trampolines, electric kiddie cars, a carousel, clown shows, jugglers and more. (By the way, the clown shows are not just for kids!)

Parque de las Palapas is also the center of activity for festivals and holy days. Come for concerts, parades and dancing during **Carnaval de Cancún**

Scan this QR code for events and activities.

IRINA BRESTER/ALAMY STOCK PHOTO

(Carnival). On **Día de Muertos** (Day of the Dead), locals fill the park with altars honoring their ancestors, as well as historical figures and deceased celebrities. Live music, parades and face painting are all part of the celebration.

Craft Market

The south side of the plaza has a market selling arts and crafts from across Mexico. Unlike the other markets in town, this one is small but well curated, with unique clothing, jewelry, woodwork and artwork made by local and national artisans.

There are usually additional vendors and artisans selling their wares at **Parque Bohemio**, one block north.

QUICK BREAK

Food stalls and mobile food carts are pretty much everywhere in Parque de las Palapas, so you'll have no problem finding something to snack on.

★ TOP EXPERIENCE

Isla Contoy

Spectacular **Isla Contoy** is an uninhabited national park and sanctuary that is an easy day trip from Cancún. About 800m at its widest point and over 8.5km long, it has dense foliage providing shelter for more than 170 bird species, including brown pelicans, olive cormorants, turkey birds, brown boobies and frigates.

MAP P32 **F1**

PLANNING TIP
To preserve the park, only 200 people can visit each day (by tour only). Book tours through Asterix *(contoytours.com; adult/child US$129/109)* or Isla Contoy Experience *(islacontoyexperience.com; adult/child US$139/109)*.

Scan this QR code for more information about Isla Contoy's ecology.

Tropical Island Paradise

One of the most popular day trips from Cancún, Isla Contoy is a national park and bird sanctuary that sits off the northern tip of the Yucatán Peninsula, marking the meeting point of the Gulf of Mexico and the Caribbean Sea. Visitors spend most of their time at the gorgeous palm-fringed beach, soaking in crystal-clear, bathtub-temperature waters. You can also follow a trail through the mangroves and hike to an observation deck to see the extent of the island.

Bring your binoculars and your beach towel. Note that insect repellent, sunblock and plastic bottles of any kind are not allowed on the island (you'll be instructed to leave them on the boat).

Wildlife Refuge

Isla Contoy provides shelter for more than 170 bird species, earning it the nickname 'bird island'. Brown pelicans and frigate birds are the most visible, but there are also red flamingos (in season), brown boobies, snowy egrets and more. Stingrays and starfish are often spotted in the shallow waters of the beach, while iguanas, snakes and crocs hang out in the mangroves and lagoons. Four

ARKADIJ SCHELL/SHUTTERSTOCK

species of sea turtle nest on Isla Contoy. Mammals are not found on the island (due to the lack of fresh water), allowing birdlife and other creatures to flourish.

Caribbean Cruise

Excursions to Isla Contoy involve a two-hour journey across azure seas, with the potential to spot dolphins. Most include a snorkel stop on the way there and a shopping stop at Isla Mujeres on the way back. Seasickness on the boats is not unheard of, so bring some medication!

Crews often cultivate a party atmosphere on the boat, with loud music and an open bar; but the island itself is pure peaceful bliss.

QUICK BREAK

Isla Contoy tours include fruit and drinks on the boat (did we mention the open bar?), in addition to a buffet lunch served on the island.

★ TOP EXPERIENCE

Isla Blanca

First things first: **Isla Blanca** is not an island, but a peninsula, stretching north from Cancún for some 25km. At the end of the road, it is barely more than a strip of sand, stretching between a shallow lagoon and the Caribbean blue. The sandy beach is miraculously void of development.

MAP P32 **F1**

PLANNING TIP
Driving can be slow going, but it's a great opportunity to soak up the scenery along the way. While swimming, watch out for potentially strong undercurrents.

A Day at the Beach

On sunny weekends and during vacation weeks, folks drive up from Cancún for family picnics, beach bonfires, shoreline walks and long days in the sun and surf. At other times, Isla Blanca is nearly deserted. It is, possibly, your only opportunity for seaside solitude on the Yucután's entire Caribbean coast. Just bring all the drinks, snacks and beach gear that you need, as there are usually no amenities here (aside from the occasional guy selling *cocos frescos*).

Kitesurfing

The beach at Isla Blanca may be deserted, but the lagoon on the west side is rarely so, at least from November to May. That's because the winds don't stop blowing during this season, so the kiteboarders are riding high. Conditions at Isla Blanca are excellent for kiters of all skill levels, but especially beginners. The water on Laguna Chacmuchuch is shallow and flat, which makes it perfect for learning and practicing new skills.

There are several kite schools at Isla Blanca, including **Icarus Kite Centre** *(kiteboardmexico.com)* and **Kitesurf Mexico** *(kitesurfmexico.com)*.

ARTURO VEREA/SHUTTERSTOCK

These two long-running operations both offer top-notch instruction, high-quality equipment and an undeniable passion for the sport.

Getting Here

To get to Isla Blanca, it's a straight shot up the Costa Mujeres road; the last 5km are unpaved and rough. If you don't have your own car, you can take a taxi, but you'll want to make advance arrangements for a pick-up, as there's no cell service out here. There's also a red *colectivo* (small bus) that runs three times a day from La Crucera in Cancún (departing at 7am, 11am and 4pm). The last *colectivo* departs Isla Blanca at around 4:40pm. Don't miss it or you'll be sleeping in the sand!

QUICK BREAK

There is a *palapa* on the beach that is sometimes open for drinks and snacks, but you'll probably want to pack a picnic (and plenty of water) for your day at the beach.

Walk Cancún Centro

Get a taste of Cancún's vibrant local culture with this walk around El Centro. This is where Cancunenses live, work and play, where plazas and parks are crowded with local folks, and where vibrant murals and inspiring monuments adorn every corner.

START	END	LENGTH
Parque de las Palapas	Avenida Náder	1km; 1 hour

1 Central Park

Quiet by day but bustling at night, **Parque de las Palapas** is the city's most dynamic gathering place, a popular venue for street food, free entertainment and cultural celebrations. Look along Calle 5 Alcatraces for fantastic murals by Colombian artist Le Dania and others.

2 Art in the Park

Take a detour one block south to **Parque del Pintor**, lined with vibrant murals. This little park has recently been a venue for masterpieces by local twin brothers Happyone and Twinone.

3 Artistic Alleyway

On the north side of the square, the **Pasarela Frida Kahlo** is a narrow walkway, strung with lights and painted with murals. The largest painting depicts the walkway's namesake artist, while others feature themes and styles that she may have inspired.

4 Festive Lanes

Back at Parque de las Palapas, stroll east along **Tulipanes**, the colorful pedestrian lanes that lead away from the park. Flags flap in the breeze and other whimsical exhibits often adorn the way. These lanes are lined with *heladerías* (ice cream parlors) and *taquerías* (taco stalls), making them a delightful place to stop for a snack and to watch the world go by.

5 City Center

Crossing Avenida Tulum, you will arrive at the **Palacio Municipal** (City Hall), overlooking a vast plaza. Look for a monument to former president Benito Juárez, who was Mexico's first indigenous president from 1858 to 1872. Another statue memorializes Roberto Gómez Bolaños, aka Chespirito, a Mexican actor and comedian who was beloved throughout Latin America. Here, also, are photogenic *letras* (letters) of Cancún (one of many set).

6 Urban Wilds

Go around the Palacio Municipal and you'll find yourself in the midst of a **jungly park**, a shady green retreat in a hot, busy city. More paintings decorate the walls.

7 Eat Street

You have arrived at **Avenida Náder**, one of El Centro's top spots for drinking and dining. Both sides of the street are lined with enticing eateries.

8 Muralismo

Continue down the west side of the street to discover more **eye-popping murals**, many with environmental themes. In the alley near Café Nader, look for *Xik'nal*, a stunning piece by local muralist Crea, as well as the uplifting, multi-textural *Bendita Vida* (Blessed Life) by Senkoe. Further south, you'll see walls painted by nationally known artists Gonzalo Areuz and Farid Rueda.

EXPERIENCES

Explore Maya History in the City

RUINS

MAP: 1 P32 F1

With the exception of Tulum, the Maya sites along the coast are less known (and less extravagant) than inland sites. Nonetheless, Maya settlements flourished up and down the Caribbean coast, thriving on maritime trade and fishing, especially during the postclassic period (approximately 1200 to 1500 CE). Several archeological sites are open for exploration right in the city.

The most impressive is **El Meco** *(inah.gob.mx; M$75)*, located about 4km north of El Centro. The centerpiece is the 12.5m **El Castillo**, the tallest pyramid in northeastern Yucatán. Other structures are equally interesting residential buildings with some surviving architectural flourishes. If you don't have your own vehicle, you can reach El Meco by taxi, or by taking a *colectivo* from La Crucera in El Centro to Punta Sam.

Additional archaeological sites are located in the **Zona Hotelera** (p52), as is the **Museo Maya** (p52), stuffed with impressive artifacts from around the peninsula.

Marvel at Murals

STREET ART

In the 1920s, the new Mexican government began commissioning works of public art to depict historic events, celebrate cultural heritage and inspire national pride. Grand murals were the medium of choice. So began Mexican Muralism, a movement defined by artists such as Diego Rivera and José Clemente Orozco.

Today murals are still a significant feature of urban culture in Mexico, and Cancún is no exception. In the 21st century dozens of artists have decorated the facades of downtown buildings, including Gonzalo Areuz, Farid Rueda and others.

Keep your eyes open during your explorations and you'll spot some eye-popping works of art, especially in the streets around **Parque de las Palapas** (p34) and the nearby **Parque del Pintor** (MAP: 2 P32 D4) and **Parque Bohemio** (p35). There are also striking pieces along the west side of **Avenida Náder** (MAP: 3 P32 E3). Learn more on the excellent **Cancún Street Art Tour** *(cityarttoursmexico.com; M$900)*, guided by local artists, who give fascinating insights into the artworks and the role of street art in Mexican culture.

Dance the Night Away the Latin Way

BAR

MAP: 5 P32 E4

If you want to get your groove on, but you can't stomach the wild nightclubs of the hotel zone, head to **La Coyota Cancún** in El Centro. It's a fabulous Mexican restaurant and mezcal bar that just happens to host the city's hottest Latin dance scene. Salsa and bachata are the *bailes* (dances) of choice, and the music starts around 10pm nightly. Come an hour early on Tuesday or Thursday for a free lesson.

Party in Queer Cancún

BAR

Nightlife in Cancún is pretty wild, and the LGBTIQ+ scene is no exception. The longest-standing gay club is **11:11** (MAP: 6 P32 **D3**; pronounced '*on*-say *on*-say'). Think drag shows, burlesque and dance nights, in addition to cheap beer and cocktails. Nearby, **Laser Hot Bar Beer & Queer** (MAP: 7 P32 **D4**) keeps the troops entertained with drag shows, karaoke and a signature laser show. Both clubs are open from 10pm Wednesday through Sunday. Look for the rainbow-colored crosswalks and you'll know you're getting close.

Even outside of the dedicated gay 'scene,' Cancún is relatively accepting of gay and lesbian couples. Normally, neither visitors nor locals will bat an eye at same-sex displays of affection.

Go Wild in the City

PARK

MAP: 8 P32 **B8**

Beloved by nature lovers and fitness fans, **Parque Kabah** is an unexpectedly dense expanse of jungle and greenery in the heart of El Centro. A 1.9km dirt trail circles through the park's lush forest, inviting runners, walkers and birders. Athletes work out at the outdoor gym and kids play at the excellent playground. No matter what you do, keep your eyes peeled for urban wildlife, especially birds, coatis and even monkeys.

SHOP 'TILL YOU DROP

Grab your shopping bag and head to the covered market, **Mercado 28** (MAP: 4 P32 **B3**), for the city's best selection of Mexican handicrafts and souvenirs.

Cancún's biggest tourist market, it has hundreds of vendors, selling everything from high-quality handicrafts to cheap rip-offs. Hammocks, hats, clothing, textiles, ceramics and silver are all on display, as are T-shirts and tequila. Look before you buy, as many different vendors are selling the same type of items. There are no posted prices; be prepared to haggle.

After you've finished your shopping (and worked up an appetite), sample one of Cancún's best selections of street food.

LISTINGS

Best Places for...

See p32 for map of locations

$ Budget $$ Midrange $$$ Top End

Eating

Breakfast

Rooster $$
9 E3
This charming resto is a good idea any time of day, but especially for breakfast. The menu is packed with irresistible egg dishes and fresh fruit juices. *7am-9pm*

Marakame Café $$
 10 D8
Pay one reasonable price for a fantastic breakfast buffet with an open mimosa bar. (No, you're not dreaming!) *8am-1am*

International Fare

El Tigre y El Toro $$
11 E3
Feast on gourmet thin-crust pizza and homemade pasta in the romantic candlelit garden on Avenida Náder. *6pm-12:30am Mon-Sat, to 11:30pm Sun*

La Fonda del Zancudo $$
 12 E2
Worth a trip just for the setting in a lovely walled patio, lit with strings of lights and lanterns. Serves an eclectic mix of pizzas, pasta and more. *5pm-midnight Mon-Sat*

Peter's Restaurante $$$
 13 F4
The simple interior belies the exquisite, sophisticated fusion fare coming out of the kitchen, courtesy of chef Peter Houben. A+ for service. *6-9:30pm Tue-Sat*

Seafood

Kiosco Verde $$
14 F1
Fabulous, fresh seafood from a beloved local restaurant that started life (in 1974, shortly after the founding of Cancún) as a grocery store and fish market. *12:30-8pm Wed-Mon*

El Pescado Ciego $$
see  11 E3
A select menu featuring tacos, pasta and grills – some seafood but some decidedly not – in a sweet spot on Avenida Náder. *2-11pm*

Puerto Santo $$$
see  14 F1
Guests rave about the outstanding service and unique combinations of flavors at this oceanfront restaurant near the Puerto Juárez ferry terminal. *noon-midnight*

Tacos

Taquería Coapeñitos $
15 E2
Warm hospitality and authentic flavors make Coapeñitos a no-fail choice for tacos and drinks. The steak and chorizo taco is a winner. *10am-1am*

Tacos Rigo $
 16 A4
A local favorite for more than three decades, famous for its tacos *al pastor* (spit-roasted pork) and festive atmosphere. Near Mercado 28. *8am-midnight*

Gory Tacos $
 17 D3
Travelers rave about the fish tacos and friendly service at this colorful stand, down the street from Parque de las Palapas. *11am-11pm*

El Socio Naiz $$
 18 E3
Sample excellent and unusual tacos (including veggie options) in the

open-air dining room. A delightfully sophisticated taco stop. *2-11pm Sun-Tue, to midnight Wed-Sat*

Yucatecan

Lonchería El Pocito $$

 B1

A fan-cooled restaurant under a *palapa* roof, with a daily changing menu of regional specialties. This is the place to sample *cochinitas pubil* (slow-roasted pork). *8am-8pm Wed-Mon*

Tuch Cantina Yucateca $$

 F7

This classy restaurant features an extensive menu of traditional regional specialties, including *pavo en relleno negro* (turkey in black stuffing) and *poc chuc* (marinated roasted pork). *1pm-1am Sun-Wed, to 2am Thu-Sat*

Drinking

Coffee

Onesto Café

 E4

Here's your hipster coffee shop, with sidewalk seating, cool music and high-quality java drinks. *9am-7pm Mon-Sat*

Cerveza

Puerto Juárez Brewery

22 F1

A breezy little brewhouse in the heart of El Centro, producing pale ales, brown ales and an oatmeal stout. *3-9:30pm Tue-Sat*

El Estadio Cervecería

 A6

Great selection of craft beers on tap, plus live music, *micheladas* (beer and tomato juice) and sports on the tube. *4pm-3am Mon-Thu, from 1pm Fri-Sun*

Good Times

Mumma Rooftop

 E2

Shoot pool, sip drinks and listen to tunes overlooking downtown Cancún. At Nomads Rooftop. *11am-2am*

Mora Mora

 A2

A cool underground venue, plastered with murals and thumping with live hip-hop, punk and metal acts. *5pm-1am Mon-Sat*

Tiki Mug

 A4

There's something for everyone at this tropical-themed bar, from cocktails to hookahs to sports on the big screen. *5pm-2am*

Shopping

Markets

Mercado 28

see 4 B3

One of the city's largest souvenir markets, with hundreds of stalls selling T-shirts, leather goods, handicrafts and tequila. Haggling is the norm, but prices are cheaper than in the Zona Hotelera.

Mercado Municipal Ki-Huic

27 E4

A small warren of stalls and shops along Av Tulum, carrying a wide variety of souvenirs and handicrafts, with a (relatively) laid-back atmosphere.

Malls

Puerto Cancún Marina Town Center

 F5

An open-air mall, with many stores, dozens of restaurants, an IMAX movie theater and sweeping views of Zona Hotelera. It's all pretty fancy, but it's not geared to tourists and there's no hard sell.

Plaza Las Américas

 E7

A vast modern shopping mall that includes department stores, a multiplex cinema and a food court.

See p54
for eating,
drinking and
shopping
listings

Explore Zona Hotelera

The beach at the Zona Hotelera is Cancún's number one attraction, and you could be forgiven for spending your entire vacation on these luxuriously soft sands. Fantastic diving and snorkeling are right offshore, including an incredible underwater sculpture museum. Beach resorts have spectacular swimming pools, delectable dining and on-site entertainment, so you never have to leave the grounds. But we don't recommend that! Curious travelers in the Zona Hotelera will also discover rich Maya history, diverse dining, fabulous entertainment and nightlife, and a wealth of opportunities to get active on and off the water.

Getting Around

Bus

The R1 and R2 buses are useful for travelers to get around the Zona Hotelera. They both run the full length of Blvd Kukulcán and continue to El Centro. The bus fare is M$12.

Airport Transportation

An ADO bus transports travelers between the airport terminals and Plaza Fiesta in the Zona Hotelera *(M$140)*. Alternatively, book a private transfer or shared shuttle in advance to avoid the overpriced services that wait at the airport. Regular taxis are not allowed to do airport pick-ups.

THE BEST

BEACH Playa Delfines (p52)

BEACH BAR Tribu Beach Club (p55)

UNDERWATER ADVENTURE Museo Subacuático de Arte (p50)

SEAFOOD Fred's Seafood & Raw Bar (p55)

BIKE TRAIL Cancún Ciclopista (p53)

Playa Delfines (p52)
BRUNO_DOINEL/SHUTTERSTOCK

A
B
C
D
E
F
1
2
3
4
0
2 km
0
1 mile
CANCÚN
Blvd Kukulcán
Av Tulum
Av Bonampak
11 Elite Cyclery – The Big Store
10 Cancún Ciclopista
14 SUP Cancún
24
Playa Linda
ZONA HOTELERA
Ferry to Isla Mujeres
Bahía de Mujeres
5 Playa Langosta
Playa Pez Volador
12 Go Kayak Cancún
15 Kianah's Sportfishing
Playa Tortugas
Laguna de Nichupté
See Enlargement
CARIBBEAN SEA
Laguna Bojórquez
28
Playa Chac-Mool
Nichupté Bridge (under construction)
22
34
6 Yamil Lu'um
25
2 Playa Marlín
35
Laguna del Amor
27
26
For more see
Top Experiences p50
Experiences p52
Eating p54
Drinking p55
Shopping p55

Tequila Tasting Experience 16
23
20
Blvd Kukulcán
8 Museo Maya
9 San Miguelito
Playa San Miguelito
La Isla
Laguna Cabra
Zona Arqueológica El Rey 7
1 Playa Delfines
Laguna Río Inglés
18
21
Blvd Kukulcán
Blvd Kukulcán
Punta Nizucd
Punta Nizuc
Museo Subacuático de Arte
Playa Caracol
Bahía de Mujeres
Ferry to Isla Mujeres
La Isla
Punta Cancún
19
Plaza Caracol
ZONA HOTELERA
Playa Gaviota Azul
4
Laguna Bojórquez
33
30
31
32
29
Playa Gaviota Azul
17
360 Surf School 13
Playa Chac Mool 3
0 500 m
0 0.25 miles
A B C D E F
5 6 7 8

★ TOP EXPERIENCE

Museo Subacuático de Arte

In 2009, the government of Mexico launched a creative project to protect the reefs near Cancún, at the same time offering visitors a wonderfully unique underwater experience. The **Museo Subacuático de Arte**, better known as MUSA, is one of the world's largest underwater art attractions.

MAP P48 **C8**

PLANNING TIP
Be aware of a US$10 marine-park fee that is usually charged separately to the price of a dive or snorkel trip.

Artificial Reefs

The exhibit features some 500 concrete sculptures, all resting on the sea floor. They are not only artworks but also artificial reefs, attracting algae, coral, fish and other sea creatures. The sculptures are intriguing in their own right, but even more marvelous is the way they're transformed by their surroundings, as coral grows and creatures take over.

Best of all, the artworks provide visitors the chance to snorkel and dive away from fragile corals, thus allowing reefs to recover from decades of overuse. Made from pH-neutral marine concrete, the statues do not harm the existing wildlife and are a harbor for fish and other marine creatures.

Snorkeling & Diving

MUSA currently has accessible exhibits in three locations. Dive trips go to **Manchones reef** near Isla Mujeres, where the sculptures rest at a depth of about 10m (pictured; underwater sculpture by Jason deCaires Taylor). Most outings include a second dive at the reef itself. The shallow depth at Manchones means that you can dive at MUSA even if you are not a certified diver. As such, a 'resort dive' requires only

Scan this QR code for tours and information.

JASON DECAIRES TAYLOR

a same-day, one-hour training session to learn the basics of diving. **Solo Buceo** *(solobuceo.com; US$110-135)* and **Scuba Cancún** *(scubacancun.com.mx; US$110-135)* are good options.

Snorkelers can see the Manchones statues from above, while other snorkel trips go to the smaller MUSA exhibit at **Punta Nizuc**, which is only 4m deep. Many tour companies offer snorkeling trips, including **Aquaworld** *(aquaworld.com.mx; US$58)*.

Glass-Bottom Boats

If you don't want to get wet, you can see the exhibits at Punta Nizuc from the comfort of a **glass-bottom boat** *(US$58)*. The journey includes a ride through the Nizuc lagoon and mangroves, in addition to the museum.

QUICK BREAK

You'll find inviting lagoon-side cafes at the hotel and marina facilities near Solo Buceo and Scuba Cancún. If you go snorkeling with Aquaworld, you can stop for lunch at **Don's Tacos & Burritos** (p54).

EXPERIENCES

Sink your Toes into the Sand BEACH

Cancún beaches are open to all-comers. The beachfront is public property, so hotels and resorts cannot restrict interlopers from frolicking in the water or lounging on the sand. However, there are only a few public access points and even fewer public beaches that offer facilities such as bathrooms and beach umbrellas.

One of the best is **Playa Delfines** (MAP: 1 P48 **C6**), a wide gorgeous beach at Km 17.5, with tantalizing water in multiple shades of blue. Arrive early in the day to take advantage of free parking and free *palapas* (thatched-roof structures). Pack your own picnic, as there is no food or drink available here.

Further north, at Km 13, **Playa Marlín** (MAP: 2 P48 **D4**) is good for warm, clear waters, powdery sand and for kids to frolic in the surf. Chairs and umbrellas are available to rent, but you should pack your own picnic.

At Km 9.5, beautiful **Playa Chac Mool** (MAP: 3 P48 **D8**) tends to be free of crowds (unlike neighboring **Playa Gaviota Azul** (MAP: 4 P48 **F7**). Umbrellas are available to rent.

Alternatively, **Playa Langosta** (MAP: 5 P48 **C1**) is located on the north side of the peninsula (sometimes called 'the top of the 7'). Calm shallow waters make it a top spot for swimming, with many beach bars nearby.

Explore Maya Sites in the City ARCHAEOLOGICAL SITE

In addition to San Miguelito, there are several Maya ruins along Blvd Kukulcán.

Perched atop a beachside knoll (supposedly at the highest point on the city's coastline), **Yamil Lu'um** (MAP: 6 P48 **D3**) features one solitary temple known as the Templo del Alácran (Scorpion's Temple). The structure – a survivor, indeed – is wedged in between the Park Royal and Westin Lagunamar hotels at Km 12.5. You must pass through one of the hotels to reach the site.

At Km 18 on Blvd Kukulcán, **Zona Arqueológica El Rey** (MAP: 7 P48 **C6**; *inah.gob.mx; M$75)* takes its name from a sculpture found at the site. It depicted a noble – possibly a *rey* (king) – wearing an elaborate headdress. The site includes a small temple and several ceremonial platforms. It was closed for construction at the time of research, but is expected to reopen in 2025.

Discover a Trove of Archaeological Artifacts MUSEUM

After visiting the ruins, head to the excellent **Museo Maya** (MAP: 8 P48 **C6**; *inah.gob.mx; M$100)* to see some of the artifacts excavated from this (and other) sites. Hundreds of items are on display, including finely crafted jewelry, especially items made from jade and obsidian, intricate pottery and many stone carvings and glyphs.

Your museum ticket includes admission to a small adjoining archaeological site, **San Miguelito** (MAP: 9 P48 **C6**). A shady path winds around a columned palace, an 8m-high pyramid and remains of houses.

Bike to the Beach

CYCLING

Wide, flat and relatively well maintained, the **Cancún Ciclopista** (MAP: 10 P48 **B1**) traverses 13km along Blvd Kukulcán, from Coral Beach in the north to Punta Nizac in the south. The trail runs along the roadway, not the coast, so it's not as lovely as it might be, but cyclists (and pedestrians) enjoy plenty of shade, glimpses of the sea and the occasional iguana for company. And of course, the big blue Caribbean beckons when you need to cool off. Many resorts have bikes available for guests; otherwise, you can rent one from **Elite Cyclery – The Big Store** (MAP: 11 P48 **A1**) near Plaza Las Américas in El Centro.

AQUATIC ADVENTURES

Go Kayak Cancún

MAP: 12 P48 **C2**

Discover the birds, wildlife and magic of the mangroves of Laguna Nichupté on a morning or sunset kayak tour.

360 Surf School

MAP: 13 P48 **D8**

Top-rated surf school on Playa Chac Mool guaranteeing you'll 'stand up and surf or your lesson is free'.

SUP Cancún

MAP: 14 P48 **B1**

All things stand-up paddleboarding, including rental, classes, tours and SUP yoga. At Hotel Imperial Las Perlas.

Kianah's Sportfishing

MAP: 15 P48 **C2**

One of many operations offering deep-sea fishing charters in search of sailfish, tuna, amberjacks, barracuda, triggerfish etc.

Sip the Magical Mexican Elixir

DISTILLERY

MAP: 16 P48 **C5**

While in Mexico, you'll have plenty of opportunities to drink tequila. We promise. But if you want to understand what you are drinking, sign on for a **Tequila Tasting Experience**. This is an opportunity to sample seven artisanal tequilas and learn all about the distillation and fermentation process. You'll finish with a new-found knowledge of, and appreciation for, Mexico's national liquor.

The 30-minute basic 'experience' takes place outdoors on a dock, overlooking the lagoon. There are also upgraded options that include a boat ride or a meal at a local restaurant.

LISTINGS

Best Places for...

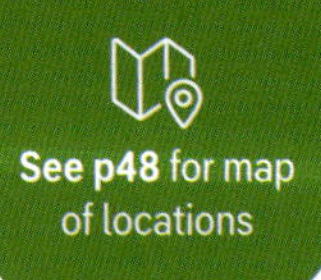
See p48 for map of locations

$ Budget $$ Midrange $$$ Top End

Eating

Affordable Fare

La Bamba $
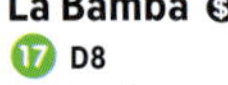
17 D8
La Bamba es *la bomba!* This under-the-radar spot gets raves for its 'Mex seafood,' especially coconut shrimp and tuna tostada. *noon-7:30pm Sun-Thu, to 9:30pm Fri & Sat*

El Galeón del Caribe $
18 C7
A local hangout at the southern end of the Zona Hotelera, serving up a short menu of ceviche, fried fish and *cocteles* (cocktails). *noon-7pm*

Mr Gory $
19 D6
The friendliest little resto in Cancún. Great spot for no-frills breakfast or lunch, made with love. *7am-5pm*

Mexican

Don's Tacos & Burritos $

20 C5
An unassuming roadside taco stop in the Zona Hotelera, with superb tacos and strong drinks, served under a *palapa* roof. *10:30am-9pm*

Surfin' Burrito $$

see 17 D8
A small space with a surfer vibe, serving build-your-own burritos. Lots of veggie and vegan options available. *8am-1am*

Navíos Mexican Fusion $$$
21 C7
This stunning lagoon-side spot specializes in unique interpretations of Mexican favorites. Come around 6pm for a spectacular sunset. *noon-10pm*

Italian

La Pizzarra $$
22 D3
Nosh on specialty pizzas and tasty pasta dishes on a wide, shady porch overlooking the lagoon. *noon-10pm*

Parole Cancún $$$

23 C5
Romantic setting on a deck extending over the lagoon. Delectable Italian fare (Wagyu meatballs!) is enhanced by snazzy presentations and live music. *5pm-1am*

Beachfront Dining

Cocos & Grill $$
24 B1
A welcoming spot for fresh seafood and cold drinks, right on the beach. *10:30am-6:30pm*

El Fish Fritanga $$

25 D4
The vibe is casual, but the food and drink are top-notch. It faces the lagoon, but the view is lovely and there are tables in the sand. *11am-11pm*

Casitas $$$

26 C4
Dine on the sand in private, breezy seaside tents. The excellent service and gorgeous setting make for a supremely romantic night out. *6:30-11pm*

Special Occasions

Fred's Seafood & Raw Bar $$$

see 16 C5

Set amid tropical gardens facing the lagoon, this contemporary restaurant wows guests with its fantastic seafood and sophisticated design. *1pm-midnight*

Harry's Cancún $$$

27 C4

A date-night favorite for its chic decor, perfectly presented seafood and steaks and flawless service. Spoiler alert: there's a sweet surprise at the end. *1pm-2am*

Lorenzillo's $$$

28 D3

You'll pay a premium for the lobster at this touristy place, but you'll get your choice of 16 different decadent preparations. Keep an eye out for crocs, which frequent this lagoon-side spot. *1-11pm*

Drinking

Beach Clubs

Tribu Beach Club

29 E7

Come for stunning seafood dishes and exceptional service in a picture-perfect location on Playa Gaviota Azul. *11am-3am*

Mandala Beach

30 E7

It's a nonstop party at Mandala Beach, which features three swimming pools, luxurious day beds, strong drinks and attentive service. *11am-5:30pm*

Coco Bongo Beach Party

 31 E7

Less of a beach party and more of a pool party, with free-flowing drinks, live entertainment and plenty of wet-and-wild fun. *1-8pm*

Nightclubs

HRoof

see 27 C4

City views, attentive service and luxe vibes guarantee that a night out at HRoof is something special. DJs spin techno, hip-hop and Latin music till the wee hours. *11pm-5am Fri & Sat*

Coco Bongo

see  31 E7

The Vegas-style show dazzles with acrobatics, tribute bands and flashy dance routines. When the show is over, the all-night dance party begins. *9pm-3am*

Señor Frog's

 32 E7

Is it hokey? Yes, yes it is. But it's hella fun, delivering live shows, silly games, conga dancing, free shots and good times. *11am-2am*

City

 33 E7

Claiming to be the largest nightclub in Latin America, this Friday-night venue has a huge central stage for drinking and dancing, surrounded by stadium-style levels for watching the action. *10:30pm-3am Fri*

Shopping

Malls

La Isla Shopping Village

 34 D3

An indoor-outdoor mall, with a network of canals, a Ferris wheel, aquarium, movie theater and boutique stores. *10am-10pm*

Plaza Kukulcán

35 D4

The largest mall in Cancún hosts temporary art exhibits, in addition to the many stores selling silverwork and other local artisanal souvenirs. *10am-10pm*

★ WORTH A TRIP

Chichén Itzá

The most famous and best restored of the Yucatán Maya sites, Chichén Itzá, while tremendously crowded, will still impress even the most jaded visitor. Stretching across 10 sq km, the once-great city is home to an astonishing array of ruins, including majestic temples and a towering pyramid.

PLANNING TIP
Chichén Itzá is always busy, but the crowds (and temperatures) are more bearable in the morning. Arrive at opening time and you'll have several hours to explore before most of the tour buses arrive.

Scan this QR code for opening times and admission prices.

El Castillo

Upon entering Chichén Itzá, **El Castillo** (aka the Pyramid of Kukulcán) rises before you in all its grandeur. The first temple here was pre-Toltec, built around 800 CE, but the present 25m-high structure, built over the old one, has the plumed serpent sculpted along the stairways and Toltec warriors represented in the doorway carvings at the top of the temple. You won't see the carvings, however, as ascending the pyramid was prohibited after a fatal accident here in 2006.

The structure is actually a massive Maya calendar formed in stone. Each of El Castillo's nine levels is divided in two by a staircase, making 18 separate terraces that commemorate the 18 20-day months of the Maya Vague Year. The four stairways have 91 steps each; add the top platform and the total is 365, the number of days in the year. On each facade of the pyramid are 52 flat panels, which are reminders of the 52 years in the Maya calendar round.

The older pyramid inside El Castillo has a red jaguar throne with inlaid eyes and spots of jade. Also lying behind the screen is a *chac-mool* (Maya sacrificial stone sculpture). The entrance to El Túnel, the passage up to the throne, is at the base of El Castillo's north side. You can't go in, though.

0 200 m
0 0.1 miles
Gran Museo de Chichén Itzá
Carretera Mérida - Puerto Juárez
MEX 180
Cenote Sagrado
Sacbé
Templo del Barbado
Gran Juego de Pelota
Plaza Principal
Plataforma de Venus
Templo de las Grandes Mesas
Western Entrance
Entrance to El Túnel
Templo de los Guerreros
Juego de Pelota
Unidad de Servicios
El Castillo (Pyramid of Kukulcán)
Grupo de las Mil Columnas
Columnata Noreste
El Osario
Juego de Pelota
Casa de los Metates
Juego de Pelota
El Mercado
Baño de Vapor
Templo del Venado
Cenote Xtoloc
La Casa Colorada
Juego de Pelota
Eastern Entrance Admissions Gate
El Caracol
Hotel Mayaland
Templo de los Tableros Esculpidos
Old Hwy
Edificio de las Monjas
Akab-Dzib
Gate
Valladolid (45km)
(14km)

IVAN SOTO COBOS/SHUTTERSTOCK

QUICK BREAK
Inside the western entrance, **Cafe 28** serves Starbucks-style drinks and muffins. For something more substantial, go for the tacos, nachos or burritos nearby at casual eatery Oxtun.

Researchers in 2015 learned that the pyramid most likely sits atop a 20m-deep cenote (natural pool), which puts the structure at greater risk of collapsing.

Grupo de las Mil Columnas

This group east of El Castillo pyramid takes its name – which means 'Group of the Thousand Columns' – from the forest of pillars stretching south and east. The star attraction is the **Templo de los Guerreros** (Temple of the Warriors; pictured), adorned with stucco and stone-carved animal deities. At the top of its steps is a classic reclining *chac-mool* figure, but ascending to it is not longer allowed.

Many of the columns in front of the temple are carved with figures of warriors. Archaeologists working in 1926 discovered a Temple of Chac-Mool lying beneath the Templo de los Guerreros.

You can walk through the columns on its south side to reach the **Columnata Noreste**, notable for the 'big-nosed god' masks on its facade. Some have been reassembled on the ground around the statue. Just to the south are the remains of the **Baño de Vapor** (Steam Bath or Sweat House) with an underground oven and drains for the water. The sweat houses (there are two on site) were regularly used for ritual purification.

Gran Juego de Pelota

The **great ball court**, the largest and most impressive in Mexico, is only one of the city's eight courts, indicative of the importance the games held here. The court, to the left of the visitor center, is flanked by temples at either end and is bounded by towering parallel walls with stone rings cemented up high. Along the walls of the ball court are stone reliefs, including scenes of decapitations of players.

There is evidence that the ball game may have changed over the years. Some carvings show players with padding on their elbows and knees, and it is thought that they played a soccer-like game with a hard rubber ball, with the use of hands forbidden. Other carvings show players wielding bats; it appears that if a player hit the ball through one of the stone hoops, their team was declared the winner. It may be that during the Toltec period, the losing captain, and perhaps their teammates as well, was sacrificed.

The court exhibits some interesting acoustics: a conversation at one end can be heard 135m away at the other, and a clap produces multiple loud echoes.

Cenote Sagrado

From the Plataforma de los Cráneos (Platform of Skulls), a 400m rough stone *sacbé* (path) runs north (a five-minute walk) to the huge sunken well that

MAGIC OF THE EQUINOX

At the vernal and autumnal equinoxes (around March 20 and September 22), the morning and afternoon sun produces a light-and-shadow illusion of the serpent ascending or descending the side of El Castillo's staircase. The illusion is almost as good in the week preceding and following each equinox (and draws much smaller crowds).

SOUND & LIGHT SHOW
For a different take on Chichén Itzá, plan an evening visit during Noches de Kukulan *(nochesde kukulkan.com. mx; M$772)*, an impressive but pricey sound and light show, held Wednesday through Sunday nights. The 25-minute event, in Spanish only, features projections on El Castillo, and you can also take a 45-minute self-guided tour around other dramatically lit parts of the ruins before the show.

gave this city its name. The **Sacred Cenote** is an awesome natural well, some 60m in diameter and 35m deep. The walls between the summit and the water's surface are ensnared in tangled vines and other vegetation.

There are ruins of a small steam bath next to the cenote.

El Caracol

Called **El Caracol** (The Snail) by the Spaniards for its interior spiral staircase, this observatory, to the south of the Ossuary, is one of the most fascinating and important of all Chichén Itzá's buildings (but, alas, you can't enter it).

In a fusion of architectural styles and religious imagery, there are Maya Chaac rain-god masks over four external doors facing the cardinal points. The windows in the observatory's dome are aligned with the appearance of certain stars at specific dates. From the dome, priests decreed the times for rituals, celebrations, corn planting and harvests.

Edificio de las Monjas

Thought by archaeologists to have been a palace for Maya royalty, the so-called **Edificio de las Monjas** (Nunnery; pictured), with its myriad rooms, resembled a European convent to the conquistadores, hence their name for the building. The building's dimensions are imposing: its base is 60m long, 30m wide and 20m high.

The construction is Maya rather than Toltec, although a Toltec sacrificial stone stands in front. A smaller adjoining building to the east, known as La Iglesia (the Church), is covered almost entirely with carvings.

Gran Museo de Chichén Itzá

Opened in 2024, the spacious, beautifully designed **Gran Museo de Chichén Itzá** houses a trove of artifacts unearthed at Chichén Itzá. Sculptures, architectural elements, figurines, pottery, jewelry and other relics are displayed in large exhibition halls that delve into Maya cosmovision, daily life, religion and human sacrifices.

Fascinating original pieces date from the site's earliest foundation (900 BCE) to its heyday more than 1000 years later. There's also a re-creation of the interior chamber atop the pyramid of Kukulkán, with reproductions of the red jaguar throne and a sculpture of the reclining god Chac Mool.

The museum is about 2.5km from the main entrance to Chichén Itzá and is best reached by private car or taxi.

GETTING THERE
First-class ADO buses from Cancún, PDC and Tulum drop you off at the entrance. The Tren Maya station is 7km from the ruins; a bus *(M$55)* connects the two.

STEFANO EMBER/SHUTTERSTOCK

See p72
for eating, drinking and shopping listings

Explore
Isla Mujeres

Many visitors skip Cancún completely and head straight for this special offshore island, where the pace slows and resorts shrink, the sand is finer and the waters are somehow even more turquoise. Isla Mujeres (Island of Women) is different in a way that resonates with many who get overwhelmed by that frenetic city on the mainland. A 40-minute ferry ride whisks you away to a land where golf carts are the main form of transportation, where relaxing on the crushed-coral beach is the main form of entertainment and where the vibe is as chill as it gets.

Getting Around

Golf Carts

Golf carts are the main mode of transportation on Isla Mujeres. They are available to rent at Rentadore Caribe or Rentador Joaquin, both near the ferry terminal.

Bicycle

The island is only about 8km from end to end, so it's small enough to get around by bicycle (also available for rental).

Taxi

The taxi base is near the ferry terminal if you want a ride to Punta Sur or to the village of Colonias, which is about 3km south.

THE BEST

BEACH CLUB Green Demon (p66)

WALKING TRAIL Punta Sur (p67)

SNORKELING SITE Manchones Reef (p70)

EXPAT HANGOUT Isla Brewing Co (p73)

UPSCALE RESTAURANT Limón (p72)

Playa Norte (p66)
NASTYA SMIRNOVA RF/SHUTTERSTOCK

Punta Norte
See Enlargement
Av Rueda Medina
Car Ferries to Punta Sam (6km)
Ferry to Puerto Juárez (10km)
Ferries to Cancún's Zona Hotelera (13km)
Airstrip
Punta Norte
Yunque Reef
Playa Pancholo
Playa Norte
Sea Hawk Divers
Zazil-Ha
Carlos Lazo
Sección Rocas
CARIBBEAN SEA
Guerrero
Lola Valentina
Pocna Dive Center
Cemetery
López Mateos
Plaza Isla Mujeres
Matamoros
Abasolo
Guerrero
El Patio
Mexico Divers
Carey Dive Center
Aqua Adventures
Madero
Hidalgo
Morelos
Malecón
Plaza
Juárez
Bravo
Allende
Av Rueda Medina
Playa Norte
Bahía de Mujeres
0 200 m
0 0.1 miles

Laguna Makax
Salina Grande
Bahía de Mujeres
CARIBBEAN SEA
Carretera Sac Bajo
Av Rueda Medina
18
30
Playa Pescador
29
15
Carretera Punta Sur
31
Kin Há 4
Playa Indios
Garrafón de Castilla 3
Beach Club
Punta Sur Walking Trail
Statue of Ixchel
Punta Sur
Temple of Ixchel
Manchones Reef
5

For more see

Top Experiences p66
Experiences p70
Eating p72
Drinking p73
Shopping p73

0 2 km
0 1 mile

A B C D E F
5 6 7 8

★ TOP EXPERIENCE

Playa Norte

With fine sands and topaz waters, the gorgeous beaches of Isla Mujeres are the island's main attraction. None are finer than Playa Norte, a 500m strip of loveliness at the island's northern end. The sand is luxuriously soft and the water is shallow, warm and impossibly blue.

MAP P64 **D2**

PLANNING TIP
Playa Norte is one of the few places along the entire Mexican Caribbean where you can watch the sun set over the sea. Bring your camera.

Scan this QR code for a map and nearby attractions.

Swimming Conditions

On Playa Norte, the crystal-clear water rarely rises above chest height, even as you wander far from shore. It also provides super-calm conditions for kayaking and paddle-boarding. On the northeastern side, the natural pools on either side of the bridge are great for soaking and relaxing.

Beach-Club Bliss

It's certainly possible to bring your own gear and drinks and set up a cozy spot in the sand, a few steps from the waves. (And many people do just that.) Or you can hunker down at a beach club, which will provide a beach chair, umbrella and sustenance, as well as bathrooms and showers. Some clubs also have a plunge pool, hammocks and more. They each have a different vibe, from laid-back to luxurious, with music, amenities and prices to match.

Green Demon *(casadeljaguar.com/green-demon)* is one of the fancier clubs, with day beds shaded by wide umbrellas. Service is excellent, drinks are strong and vibes are positive. **Mayan Beach Club** *(mayanbeachclub.com)* also gets rave reviews for food, drinks and service. Most clubs charge a fee or require a minimum food and drink purchase (usually around M$500 per person) for use of a lounge chair.

★ TOP EXPERIENCE

Punta Sur

At the island's southern end, Punta Sur *(M$100)* is an interesting and scenic diversion when you need a break from the beach. This is the Yucatán Peninsula's highest point and the easternmost point in Mexico, and it was a sacred place for the Maya.

MAP P64 **E8**

The Goddess Ixchel

At this southern tip, the Maya built a temple dedicated to Ixchel, goddess of the moon, fertility and childbirth. Women would come to seek blessings for healthy pregnancies and successful births. They often left small sculptures of female figures as offerings to Ixchel.

Centuries later, Francisco Fernández de Córdoba stumbled upon the island in 1517. He found many artifacts depicting Ixchel and the female form, and thus dubbed the place Isla Mujeres (Island of Women). Nowadays, a **statue of Ixchel** greets you near the entrance of this national park.

PLANNING TIP
Early risers can catch a spectacular sunrise from Punta Sur, the easternmost point on the island (and Mexico).

Temple to Ixchel

Walking paths wind through the park, past colorful statues highlighting other Maya gods and historic figures. The centerpiece is the ruin of the **Temple of Ixchel**, high atop a cliff, with waves crashing below. The structure is small, but the setting is stunning.

Cliff Walk

If you can't get enough of these eye-popping limestone cliffs and turquoise waters, take a longer walk along the cliffs just outside the park. Pick up the **walking trail** near the Punta Sur parking lot. It runs along the eastern shoreline for about 1.3km until meeting the main road.

Bike Isla Mujeres

Cycle around Isla Mujeres for an overview of its intriguing history and magnificent scenery. This scenic loop takes you away from the touristy northern end, through the community of Colonias all the way to the southern tip at Punta Sur. Circle back along the eastern shore for gorgeous views of seaside cliffs and crashing surf.

START	END	LENGTH
Ferry terminal	Ferry terminal	15km; 1½ hours

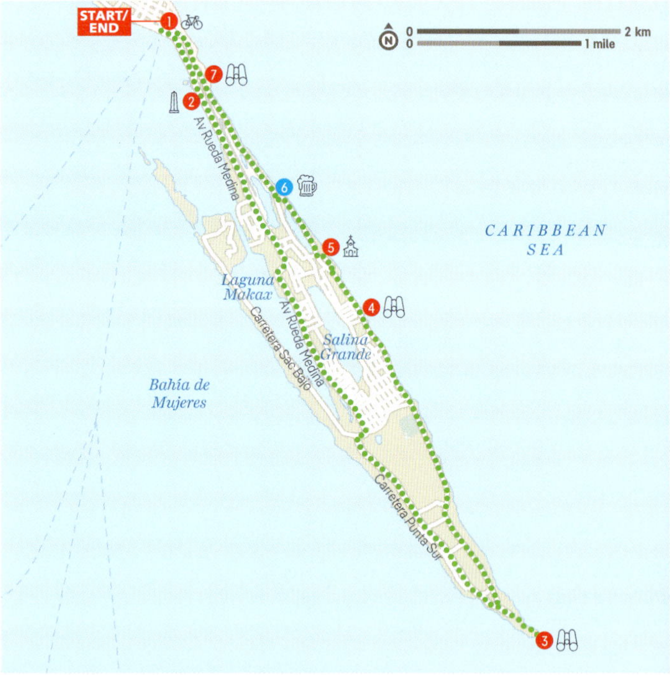

1 Bicycle Pickup

If you have just arrived at the ferry terminal, you can rent a bicycle across the street at **Rentadore Caribe** *(M$80/300 per hour/day)*. From here, head south out of town on Avenida Rueda Medina, with views across the water to Cancún on your right.

2 Emblem of an Island

You'll soon pass a **statue of a whale shark**, welcoming you to the island. From June to September, whale sharks congregate in the Afuera, or 'outside', the deep waters north of the island. Whale sharks are sharks, not whales! They are the biggest fish in the sea (up to 12m), and these gentle creatures have long been a source of wealth and pride for islanders – and a symbol of Isla Mujeres. See p70 for information about swimming with whale sharks.

3 Southern Exposure

Continue about 6.2km, skirting Laguna Makax on your right, until you reach **Punta Sur**. Take a break here to take in the stunning scenery, interesting history and ancient ruins – and perhaps an ice cream. You must leave your bicycle outside the gate.

4 Scenic Overlook

Departing the park, turn right out of the parking lot and head north. You'll pedal about 5km along the coastal road, with incredible views along the way. Make a photo stop at **Mirador Payo Obispo**, with its playful sculptures of sea creatures.

5 Seaside Chapel

Stop in the village of Colonias to visit the seaside **Capilla de Guadalupe**. This delightful chapel is dedicated to the Virgin of Guadalupe, with a shell-studded altar and stunning views out to sea. The Virgin of Guadalupe refers to an apparition of the Virgin Mary, that appeared to an indigenous Nahua man, Juan Diego, near Mexico City in 1531. She is one of Mexico's most revered religious and national symbols. From here, it's another 1.5km into town.

6 Beer Garden

If all that cycling has made you thirsty and hungry, here's your chance to stop for a burger and a beer at **Isla Brewing Co**. Enjoy a small but excellent selection of craft brews and delicious food on the delightful shady patio.

7 Last Lookout

After passing the airstrip, there's one last glorious **scenic viewpoint**, featuring rocks, sea, sky and little else. At the next intersection, turn left to return to Avenida Rueda Medina and you have completed your circumnavigation of Isla Mujeres.

EXPERIENCES

Stroll Avenida Hidalgo AREA

Avenida Hidalgo is a pedestrian-only lane that runs the length of the town center, from the plaza all the way to the beach clubs on the north side. Look for tasty food, strong beverages and ample shopping opportunities, all on an easy, fun, colorful meander. Starting in the late afternoon, many bars and restaurants lure in customers with two-for-one specials and live music. **El Patio** (MAP: 1 P64 **E3**) is a favorite, as is **Lola Valentina** (MAP: 2 P64 **D3**).

It's a great chance to do your souvenir shopping, with many shops in one place and prices generally cheaper than in Cancún. Most items are not made on the island, but there's a great selection of Mexican handicrafts, tequila and other items of interest, ranging from hammocks to textiles, silver and jewelry. Vendors are not shy with the hard sell, so don't be afraid to browse without buying. It's also fine to haggle, especially for big-ticket items.

Frolic with the Fish SNORKELING

Let us be the first (of many) to tell you that the Mesoamerican Reef is the second-largest reef system in the world, stretching from the Yucatán down to Honduras. Isla Mujeres is a superb jumping-off point for snorkeling, diving and otherwise exploring this underwater world. In fact, at the southern end of the island, you can snorkel right off the shore at **Garrafón de Castilla** (MAP: 3 P64 **D8**; *tasteofisla .com/garrafon-de-castilla; US$10*) or **Kin Há** (MAP: 4 P64 **D7**; *kinhaislamujeres.com; minimum purchase M$300*) beach clubs. Snorkel gear is available at both clubs.

Alternatively, snorkel tours *(US$50-60)* go offshore to **Manchones Reef** (MAP: 5 P64 **C8**), a vibrant area where you can spot stingrays, sea turtles, nurse sharks and colorful angelfish and parrotfish. Snorkel tours also visit Museo Subacuático de Arte (MUSA; p50) to view the fantastic underwater sculptures from above.

WHALE SHARK RULES

When swimming with whale sharks, take care to follow the rules for your own safety and that of the fish. Only three people (including the guide) can swim with a whale shark at any given time. Do not jump into the water. Enter slowly and minimize the splash. Wear a life jacket. Do not dive underneath the whale shark. Stay at least 5m from the whale shark. Do not touch or otherwise harass the creature. Do not wear sunscreen. Do not use flash photography.

Swim with Whale Sharks

SNORKELING

From June to September, whale sharks congregate in the deep waters about 35km north of Isla Mujeres. They come to feast on the eggs of the Bonito tuna that spawn here. Diving is prohibited, but you can swim and snorkel with the whale sharks *(US$150-170)*. Indeed, frolicking in the water with these gentle giants is an awe-inducing experience. There are generally more sharks in the area in July and August, which means more shark love to go around.

Dive Deeper

SCUBA DIVING

Protected by a national marine park, **Manchones Reef** is just off the coast of Isla Mujeres, featuring about 800m of vibrant reef as well as MUSA's largest underwater sculpture gallery. At an average depth of 10m, Manchones is a popular dive destination for all levels, but also an ideal place to learn. (Note that it's possible to scuba dive here even if you are not a certified diver. All local dive shops offer this option for beginners.)

Tavos Reef and **Media Luna** are other popular destinations for scuba divers, for their beautiful swim-through arches and tunnels. A unique dive site for shark lovers is **Sleeping Sharks Cave**, which is exactly what it sounds like. Several species of sharks like to take their siesta here, due to the high oxygen content of the water in the cave. A two-tank dive ranges from US$115 to US$155, depending on the destination.

DIVE SHOPS

All of the island dive shops offer snorkel and whale-shark tours, as well as dive trips.

Sea Hawk Divers

MAP: 6 P64 **D2**

Bonnie and Ariel started renting snorkel equipment on the beach back in 1985. This family-run operation is the island's longest-running dive shop.

Carey Dive Center

MAP: 7 P64 **D3**

Owner and instructor Gilberto and his crew get rave reviews for professionalism and patience.

Aqua Adventures

MAP: 8 P64 **E3**

Two decades of experience diving and snorkeling on island reefs and wrecks.

Pocna Dive Center

MAP: 9 P64 **E2**

Efficient operation with knowledgeable instructors and guides, at Selina Hostel.

Mexico Divers

MAP: 10 P64 **E3**

Sport-fishing and sailfish tours, in addition to snorkel and dive trips.

LISTINGS

Best Places for...

See p64 for map of locations

$ Budget $$ Midrange $$$ Top End

Eating

Breakfast

Mango Café $$
 C4
This colorful cafe in Colonias (mid-island) draws crowds for its coconut French toast and other Caribbean-inspired fare. *7am-3pm*

Rooster $$
 D3
Hearty breakfast dishes and refreshing smoothies served all day. *7am-5pm*

Cafe Mogagua $$
13 F4
All your brekkie favorites are here, from pancakes and eggs to *chilaquiles* (fried tortillas) and *huevos rancheros* (fried eggs in red and green salsa). Also carry-out coffee for your ferry ride. *7am-10:30pm*

Lunch

Beachin' Burrito $$
 D2
Perfect for a beach picnic – choose from six signature burritos and wash it down with freshly squeezed lemonade. *10am-4pm Thu-Tue*

Casa del Tikinxic $$
 C6
A beachfront restaurant serving the Yucatecan specialty *tikin xic* (marinated fish cooked in banana leaves) and other fantastically fresh seafood. *10:30am-7pm*

Dinner Dates

Olivia $$$
16 E3
Feast on a fusion of flavors from Greece, Morocco and Turkey on a delightful patio. *5-9:45pm Mon-Sat Nov-Apr, Tue-Sat May-Oct*

Rosa Sirena's $$$
 C4
Set on a breezy rooftop in Colonias, this is a colorful destination for modern Mexican fare, especially seafood. Also cocktails, dessert and live music. *5-10pm Tue-Sun*

Limón $$$
 C6
Chef Sergio serves up fantastic Mexican dishes with international flair, all in an intimate courtyard in Colonias. The lobster Sergio is divine. *4-11pm Mon-Fri*

Lola Valentina $$$
see  D3
A sophisticated destination on Avenida Hidalgo. Come for a tasty Mexi-Carib dinner, or swing into the bar for craft cocktails. *8am-11pm*

Beach Clubs

Zama Beach Club $$
 C3
With a plunge pool and various beach-lounging choices, this is a great option at Playa Central, especially when it's too windy on Playa Norte. *8am-10pm*

Kin Há $$$
see  D7
This south-end spot has a long menu of seafood (and other) delights, including the specialty lobster *tikin xic*.

Green Demon $$$
 D1
Swanky spot on Playa Norte, with luxurious shaded day beds and fantastic service. Sandwiches,

salads and ceviche are on the menu. *10am-7pm*

Mayan Beach Club

$$$

 D2

Top marks for delicious seafood and attentive service, as well as a lovely pool area if you need a break from the beach. *8am-10pm*

Drinking

Coffee

Coffee Break

 E3

Fantastic cold coffee drinks and frappes, plus fresh pastries and made-to-order baguette sandwiches. *8am-4pm Mon-Sat*

Café El Palmar

 E3

The destination for coffee aficionados. The beans are grown on a family farm in Chiapas, then roasted and blended for maximum flavor. *7:30am-8:30pm Mon-Sat, to 3pm Sun*

Bambu Cafe

 E2

Rich coffee, healthy smoothies and tempting baked goods and sandwiches in a secret garden out back. *7am-3pm*

Beach Bars

Lima & Coco

 D2

A delightful 'fruit bar' on Playa Norte, with fabulous smoothies, fresh juices, cocktails and food. *11am-7pm*

Tiny Gecko

 F4

On the less-traveled east side of the island, this groovy spot offers cheap drinks, live music and ocean breezes. True to its name, the place is tiny. And there are geckos. *8:30am-11pm Mon-Sat*

Tarzan

 D2

Cold drinks, reggae music and super-chill vibes. Beach chairs available to rent. *9am-7pm*

Beyond the Beach

Isla Brewing Co

 C4

Isla's own microbrewery, serving up blondes and pale ales (and excellent food) on a shady patio in Colonias. *noon-9pm Mon-Sat*

Joint

 C6

Travelers love this jungle bar for cold beers, frozen mojitos and live reggae music seven days a week. Cash only. *10am-9pm*

El Patio

see  E3

A favorite among expats for its two-for-one happy-hour specials and live music into the night. *4:30pm-midnight*

Shopping

Arts & Crafts

Women's Beading Cooperative

30 D6

Unique and beautiful jewelry, designed and crafted by the women of the Island of Women. Near Punta Sur. *9am-5pm Mon-Sat, 10am-2pm Sun*

Nalu Gallery

31 D7

This sweet gallery offers a diverse collection of pottery, paintings and jewelry, with a ceramic studio out back and the delightful Ulan Eatery across the street. *9am-9pm Mon-Sat*

Aztlán Galería

 E3

Isla originals! Hand-carved masks and figurines, as well as custom-designed tees and other unusual souvenirs. *noon-9pm*

See p84
for eating, drinking and shopping listings

Explore Isla Holbox

Two hours north of Cancún, Isla Holbox once attracted only windsurfers and beach bums. Now its swanky swing bars, beachfront yoga and lobster pizza call to travelers of all ages and interests (including windsurfers and beach bums). Quirky and cool, Holbox is morphing into something of a 'Tulum North', with a diverse and delicious food scene, low-key but fun nightlife, and independent and adventurous clientele. Best of all, the entire island is part of the vast Yum Balam nature reserve, protecting 150 species of birds (flamingos!), as well as migrating whale sharks (which you can see if you come at the right time).

Getting Around

Ferries

To get here, take an ADO bus or a private van to the port at Chiquilá. (You can get transportation from Cancún airport or El Centro.) Two ferry companies make the 30-minute trip to the island: 9 Hermanos and Holbox Express. Buy tickets online or at the point of departure.

Car

There are none! The island is mostly walkable (except when it floods after heavy rains).

ATV

Four-wheel drive taxis roam the so-called streets and wait at the ferry terminal.

THE BEST

TOUR Sunrise kayak tour (p83)

WILDLIFE SIGHTING Whale sharks (p82)

NATURAL PHENOMENON Bioluminescence (p82)

BREAKFAST SPOT Mr Happy (p84)

BEACH CLUB Punta Caliza (p84)

Sunset on Isla Holbox

JORDAN FOX/ALAMY STOCK PHOTO

A B C D

1 2 3 4 5 6

0 400 m
0 0.2 miles

For more see

Top Experiences p78
Experiences p82
Eating p84
Drinking p85
Shopping p85

GULF OF MEXICO

5 Kukulkite

Av Damero
Av Pedro Joaquín Caldwell
C Sierra
C Carito
C Palomino
C Gerónimo de Aguilar
C Paseo Kuka
See Enlargement
C Tiburón Ballena
C Hernán Cortez
C Porfirio Díaz
C Esmedregal
C Canane
C Tintorera
C Lisa
21 26 6 7 8 3 18

Aeródromo de Holbox

A B C D

E
F
G
H
1
2
3
4
5
6
17
23
Punta Mosquito
Av Damero
15
C Paseo Kuka
Playa Holbox
16
Av Damero
C Paseo Kuka
13
C Paseo Kuka
C Gerónimo de Aguilar
GULF OF MEXICO
14
Av Pedro Joaquín Caldwell
C Sierra
20
27
4
11
Holbox Kiteboarding School
Azul Tourquesa
2
22
Av Pedro Joaquín Caldwell
25
9
C Tiburón Ballena
24
29
10
19
Av Damero
C Carito
28
12
C Porfirio Díaz
C Palomino
K'íiwik Central Park
0
100 m
C Carito
VIP Holbox
1
C Palomino
C Carito
Bahía de Holbox

★ TOP EXPERIENCE

Punta Mosquito

Northeast of town, **Punta Mosquito** is the 'elbow' of Isla Holbox, a pristine place where the island's swamps and mangroves meet the sea. At low tide, the sandbar off the point becomes a magnificent, vast, beachy expanse – a spectacular seascape of sand, sky and sparkling sea.

MAP P76 **H1**

PLANNING TIP
Check the tide charts. During high tide (and high winds), water levels rise, so you might end up wading through several feet of water to reach the sandbar.

Scan this QR code for information about the Yum Balam protected area.

Yum Balam Nature Reserve

Punta Mosquito is protected by **Yum Balam**, a nature reserve that was established in 1994 at the urging of the local community. The reserve protects the surrounding wetlands and mangrove forests, which provide sanctuary for prolific wildlife. Birdlife is rich, with pelicans, ospreys, spoonbills and flamingos (in season; pictured). The point is also home to reptiles such as sea turtles, iguanas, snakes and crocodiles.

Note that entrance to this area is prohibited to protect the animals as well as the humans. (Did we mention the crocs?)

The Sandbar

Curious and adventurous travelers can walk out along the sandbar to the edge of the restricted area (which is clearly marked). At low tide, the sandbar becomes a magnificent, vast expanse, surrounded by crystal-clear waters. Wading birds congregate in the shallows, and you can also spot starfish, stingrays and other fish. It's an idyllic destination for sunbathing, soaking and solitude. Come early in the day to beat the tour boats.

JANA HAKE/SHUTTERSTOCK

The Journey

To reach the sandbar, hike or bike to Hotel Las Nubes, which is on the beach, 2km northeast of town. From here you have to wade out to the sandbar. Walk along the sandbar for another 2km to the edge of the restricted area. The sandbar is usually well exposed at low tide, but you may be wading through a few inches (or feet) of water, depending on the tides and the winds.

If you don't want to make the wet trek, you can also get here by boat. It is one of the three stops on the popular Tres Islas tour, which is offered by every tour company in town.

QUICK BREAK
Contrary to what you might think, there is no beer served at the sandbar. Bring your own water, snacks and drinks.

Walk Isla Holbox

The tiny town of Holbox is just 1 sq km at its core, with some resorts and restaurants strung along the beach at either end. A little hippy haven, it's rich with street art, seafood and beachy haunts, and it's all walkable. Spend a few hours discovering the artistic charm and understated luxury of this island outpost.

START	END	LENGTH
K'iiwik Central Park	Las Hamacas	2km; 3 hours

0 400 m
0 0.2 miles
GULF OF MEXICO
END
6
Av Damero
C Paseo Kuka
5
Av Pedro Joaquín Caldwell
2
3
Av Damero
C Carito
C Sierra
C Palomino
4
1
START
Av Damero
C Porfirio Díaz
C Gerónimo de Aguilar
C Tiburón Ballena
C Palomino
C Carito
C Paseo Kuka
C Hernán Cortez

1 Central Park

Start your tour at the sweet central plaza, aka **K'íiwik Central Park**. This is a hub of Holbox local life, from weekend markets to late-night soccer games. Events often take place on the small, centerpiece *concha acústica* (band-shell stage). Check out the colorful and evocative mural that covers the interior.

2 Photo Ops

Stroll two blocks north and you'll reach the waterfront, where palms sway in the breeze and boats tie up on the shore. Here are the requisite Holbox *letras* (letters) so you can snap a photo to prove you were here. Behind the *letras*, the **Muelle Tiburón Ballena** (Whale Shark Pier) stretches out into the Gulf of Mexico, providing a perfect place to watch the sunset. (Bring your own beverage of choice.) A bold Maya-style monster mask is painted on the hut at the foot of the pier.

3 Beach Party

Always a local favorite, **Capitán Capitán** is one of many beach clubs that line the sandy waterfront. Excellent food, affordable drinks and top-notch service are the hallmarks of this spot. Guests also love the repurposed boat bar and the romantic two-person swing facing the sea. Great vibes all around.

4 Art Street

Leave the beach behind (momentarily) and walk up **Calle Carito**. This is the island's most colorful and artistic avenue, with murals adorning almost every building on the first few blocks. The artworks depict Maya and Mexican cultural themes, local personalities and a few whimsical masterpieces.

5 Beach Bliss

Back at the ocean's edge, **Playa Holbox** stretches out (seemingly endlessly) to the northeast. With soft white sand and warm turquoise waters, this is your perfect beach walk, any time of day. Stroll along the water's edge to admire the seascape, feel the ocean breeze and sink your toes into sand and surf. At any point, you can stop for a dip in the world's biggest saltwater swimming pool.

6 Las Hamacas

Beach clubs are lined up along the sand for more than 1km, and you might stop at any of them to swim, sunbathe or sip a cold beverage. We recommend **Las Hamacas** for its incredible food and private setting near the far end of the beach. Plus, it requires a 20-minute walk to get here, so you've definitely earned your R&R (and your Mezcalita cocktail).

EXPERIENCES

Swim with Whale Sharks
SNORKELING

MAP: 1 P76 **E6**

Part of Yum Balam nature preserve, the waters around Isla Holbox protect one of the largest populations of whale sharks on the planet. During summer months (generally, May to September), they come to feed in these plankton-rich waters. During this season, whale-shark tours take boatloads of people to swim and snorkel with these amazing creatures.

Tours are usually a full-day experience, including several hours on the boat (take your Dramamine!), the shark viewing, a snorkel stop and a beach picnic lunch (with fresh ceviche). Finally – tired and thrilled – you'll return in the late afternoon with memories and hopefully photos that will last a lifetime. Book through **VIP Holbox** *(vipholbox.com; M$3200)*.

Brighten Your Night with Bioluminescence
OUTDOORS

When conditions are right, the waters around Isla Holbox sparkle with neon-blue magic. This incredible natural phenomenon is caused by bioluminescent phytoplankton, which generate an iridescent glow when they are disturbed. In the right conditions, the ocean glows with every wave or ripple. A wave breaks, a foot splashes, a fish jumps – all these can trigger this otherworldly light show.

Bioluminescence is visible year-round on Holbox, but the best season is summer. The darker the skies, the better, so the new moon is ideal. Many companies organize nighttime outings to experience this phenomenon by kayaking or snorkeling. Book with **Azul Tourquesa** (MAP: 2 P76 **F5**; *azultourquesa.com.mx; M$800*), located in the Choza Pink on the beach.

MEET THE WHALE SHARKS

Does the thought of swimming with a 15-ton, 12m shark make you uneasy? Understandable, but it needn't. Gentle whale sharks feed by opening their mouths and taking in large quantities of fish, plankton and krill, much like their namesakes, whales. Of course, whales are mammals but whale sharks are sharks, aka fish, because they have gills and can breathe underwater.

Seeing and swimming with whale sharks in the wild can be an incredible experience, engendering awe for our planet and its incredible creatures. But it can also be disheartening. In some cases, there might be dozens of boats circling around a few sharks, surely causing distress. See p70 for an overview of regulations about swimming with whale sharks.

You don't necessarily need to take a tour to light up your night. You can also walk or take a taxi to **Punta Coco** (MAP: 3 P76 **A6**), about 2km west of town, where the bioluminescence is at its brightest, and see it from the beach.

Paddle Through the Mangroves KAYAKING

Behind the beaches, Holbox is a network of estuaries and lagoons, weaving through lush forests of red and black mangroves. Protected by Yum Balam reserve, this rich wildlife habitat is home to more than 200 species of birds, including the famous pink flamingos (from April to October). American crocodiles also lurk in these brackish waters. Besides providing a habitat for countless creatures, mangroves stabilize the shoreline and limit erosion. This species also plays a role in controlling climate change, storing more carbon dioxide (per unit) than any other ecosystem on earth.

Mangroves take root directly in the mucky water, so the only way to explore this unique habitat is by paddling through it, either in a kayak or on a stand-up paddleboard. **Azul Tourquesa** (see left page) offers an excellent three-hour paddle tour with a naturalist guide, either in the early morning or late afternoon for optimal wildlife sightings.

Get Blown Away KITESURFING

You won't be long on Holbox before you notice the powerful winds blowing in from the east and northeast. This strong, consistent wind (250 days a year) makes for ideal conditions for kiteboarding and its newer derivations, foil-boarding and wingfoiling. The warm flat waters don't hurt, either. The action goes down at the sandbar north of town. If you're into it, you can rent gear or take lessons through **Holbox Kiteboarding School** (MAP: 4 P76 **H4**; *holboxkiteboarding.com*) or **Kukulkite** (MAP: 5 P76 **D3**; *kukulkite.com*).

Eat Your Way Around the Island FOOD

If you like tacos (and who doesn't?), you will love the **Taco Tour Holbox** *(tacotourholbox.com; US$94)*, a fabulous, fun evening of food and drink with local taco expert Lorena De Leon. The tour includes four taco stops, showing off different flavors, venues and dining experiences (as well as paired drinks). Along the way, Lorena shares her anecdotes and expertise about the role of tacos in Mexican culture, how to make and eat tacos, and more.

LISTINGS

Best Places for...

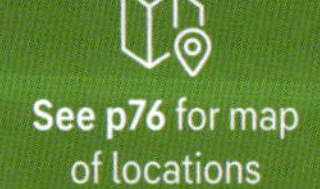

$ Budget $$ Midrange $$$ Top End

Eating

Breakfast & Lunch

Le Jardin $
6 B5
French pastries and rich coffee, served in an airy *palapa* (thatched-roof structure, surrounded by plumeria and butterflies. *8:30am-12:30pm Wed-Sun*

Zonnebloem $
7 B5
The namesake sunflowers and other blooms are bursting all over this very sweet, very small breakfast nook. *8am-5pm*

Mr Happy $$
8 B6
Relaxing in this sleek, open-air resto, feasting on satisfying egg dishes and smoothies and listening to groovy tunes, you'll be Mr Happy, too. *8am-5pm*

Painapol $$
9 F5
Trendy spot with an impressive lineup of healthy, delicious smoothies, fabulous salads, sandwiches, coffee and more. *8am-3pm Wed-Mon*

Seafood & More

Restaurante de Pimienta $
10 G5
This colorful place on the central plaza is owned by local fisherfolk, promising the freshest seafood in traditional dishes, especially *cocteles* (seafood cocktails) and *aguachiles* (raw shrimp with salsa). *noon-8pm Thu-Tue*

Barba Negra $$
11 H4
A cool and contemporary spot for seafood tacos – fish, shrimp or octopus – with your choice of four signature sauces. *1-10:30pm*

Roots Pizza a Leña $$
12 H5
Wood-fired pizza with tantalizing toppings – *mole poblano* or succulent lobster. Mexican beer on tap and 150 varieties of mezcal. *noon-11pm*

Punta Caliza $$$ 
13 E3
Intimate, open-air affair, offering sophisticated presentations of authentic Mexican flavors. Don't miss the signature seafood soup. *7am-10pm*

Beach Clubs

Capitán Capitán $
14 G4
This classic beach bar offers friendly service, a laid-back atmosphere, satisfying food, cheap drinks and no minimum charge. Can't beat it. *11am-11pm*

Mantarraya $
15 G2
Enjoy authentic Mexico vibes, with large portions of fresh seafood, Latin music and plastic furniture. *11am-6pm*

Punta Caliza $$
16 F2
Feast on shrimp tacos and other fabulous food, sip *mezcalitas* and lounge in the sun (or shade) facing the beautiful blue. *10am-7:30pm*

Las Hamacas $$
17 H1
Located toward the beach's north end, where the sand is clean and the crowds are sparse.

Wonderful food and top-notch service. Minimum purchase required to use the beach beds. *8am-10:30pm*

Maruva Beach Club $$$

18 A6

A beautiful spot at the quiet west end of the beach, surrounded by palms. Sample the unique Nikkei (Japanese-Peruvian fusion) cuisine. M$500 minimum. *8am-7pm*

Drinking

Craft Cocktails & Ales

Crónicas Taproom

19 G5

A rooftop bar with a dozen Mexican beers on tap, plus wood-fired pizzas and craft cocktails. *4-11pm*

Luuma

20 H4

A romantic tapas and cocktail bar in a palm-tree garden, lit by lanterns and candlelight. *5pm-midnight*

Live Entertainment

Tribu Bar

21 A5

There's something going on – often live music – almost every night of the week. The Sunday night jam sessions are legendary. *7pm-1am Tue-Sun*

Hot Corner

22 F5

True to its name, this popular spot occupies a busy corner in the center of town. Music blasts from the open-air stage, inspiring dancing in the sandy streets. *1pm-2am*

Aldea Kuká

23 H1

One exciting entertainment alternative is the nightly fire and acrobatic show at this outdoor venue. The restaurant is pricey, but the acrobatics and fire stunts are free. *show 8:30pm*

La Combi

24 F5

You can't miss this colorful spot with a VW van seemingly zooming out over the bar. Music, drinks and sports on the tube. *1:30pm-1am*

Caffeine Fix

Clandestino Café

25 F5

Fuel up with coffee – iced or hot – accompanied by fresh pastries and speedy wi-fi. *8am-6pm*

Copal Café

26 A5

Expertly prepared espresso drinks are served on the gorgeous palm-shaded patio, with a tempting breakfast or brunch menu. *7am-8pm*

Shopping

Fashion

Le Bazaar Boutique

27 H4

A haven for high-end, beach-inspired fashion. Shop in the plein air for flowy boho-chic clothing and stylish home decor, much of it created by Mexican designers. *10am-11:30pm*

Art Galleries

Barro Azul

28 H5

A wonderful selection of classy, contemporary artwork, especially beautiful ceramics and unique graphic art, with pieces from all around Mexico. *10am-11pm*

Holbox Galería de Arte

29 G5

An artist-owned gallery, showcasing paintings of fish, wildlife, landscapes, seascapes, and scenes and signs of life in Holbox. *10am-11pm*

See p96
for eating,
drinking and
shopping
listings

Explore Playa del Carmen

Playa del Carmen ranks right up there with Tulum as one of the Riviera's trendiest spots. Sitting coolly on the lee side of Cozumel, the town's golden beaches are packed with fit sun worshippers who enjoy easy access from the hotels, restaurants and bars on and around nearby Quinta Avenida. Coral reefs lie just offshore, while idyllic cenotes (limestone sinkholes) are an easy drive from town. Once a small fishing village, Playa, as it's known locally, today boasts a population topping 300,000. It's also one of Mexico's most cosmopolitan destinations, with visitors and expats from every corner of the globe.

Getting Around

Bus

Handily located along Quinta Avenida, the ADO Terminal Turística is where many long-distance buses arrive and depart.

Walking

The center of Playa is ideal for exploring on foot, with a dense concentration of shops, restaurants and bars along a 2km stretch of pedestrianized Quinta Avenida starting from the ferry terminal.

Bicycle

Quinta Avenida, beyond Calle 38, is a peaceful lane for pedaling your way to northern beaches (such as Punta Esmeralda). Many places rent bikes, including Cool Bikes.

THE BEST

BEACH Punta Esmeralda (p94)

CENOTE Parque Dos Ojos (p90)

MUSEUM Museo Frida Kahlo Riviera Maya (p95)

SEASIDE DINING Fusion (p97)

GARDEN RESTAURANT La Cueva del Chango (p96)

Water activities (p95), Playa del Carmen
IURII DZIVINSKYI/SHUTTERSTOCK

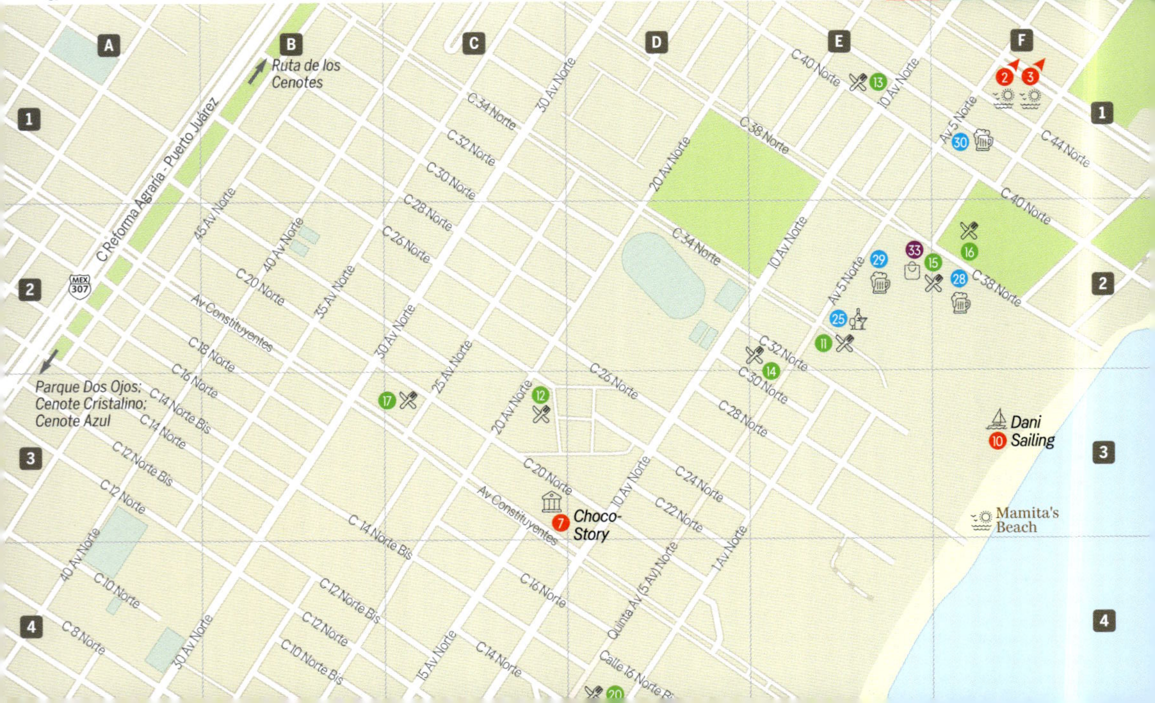

A B C D E F
1 2 3 4

Ruta de los Cenotes
C Reforma Agraria - Puerto Juárez
MEX 307
Parque Dos Ojos; Cenote Cristalino; Cenote Azul
C 44 Norte
C 40 Norte
C 38 Norte
C 34 Norte
C 32 Norte
C 30 Norte
C 28 Norte
C 26 Norte
C 24 Norte
C 22 Norte
C 20 Norte
C 18 Norte
C 16 Norte
C 14 Norte Bis
C 14 Norte
C 12 Norte Bis
C 12 Norte
C 10 Norte Bis
C 10 Norte
C 8 Norte
Calle 16 Norte Bis
Av 5 Norte
Quinta Av (5 Av) Norte
1 Av Norte
10 Av Norte
15 Av Norte
20 Av Norte
25 Av Norte
30 Av Norte
35 Av Norte
40 Av Norte
45 Av Norte
Av Constituyentes
2 3 Punta Esmeralda
7 Choco-Story
10 Dani Sailing
Mamita's Beach
11 12 13 14 15 16 17 20 25 28 29 30 33

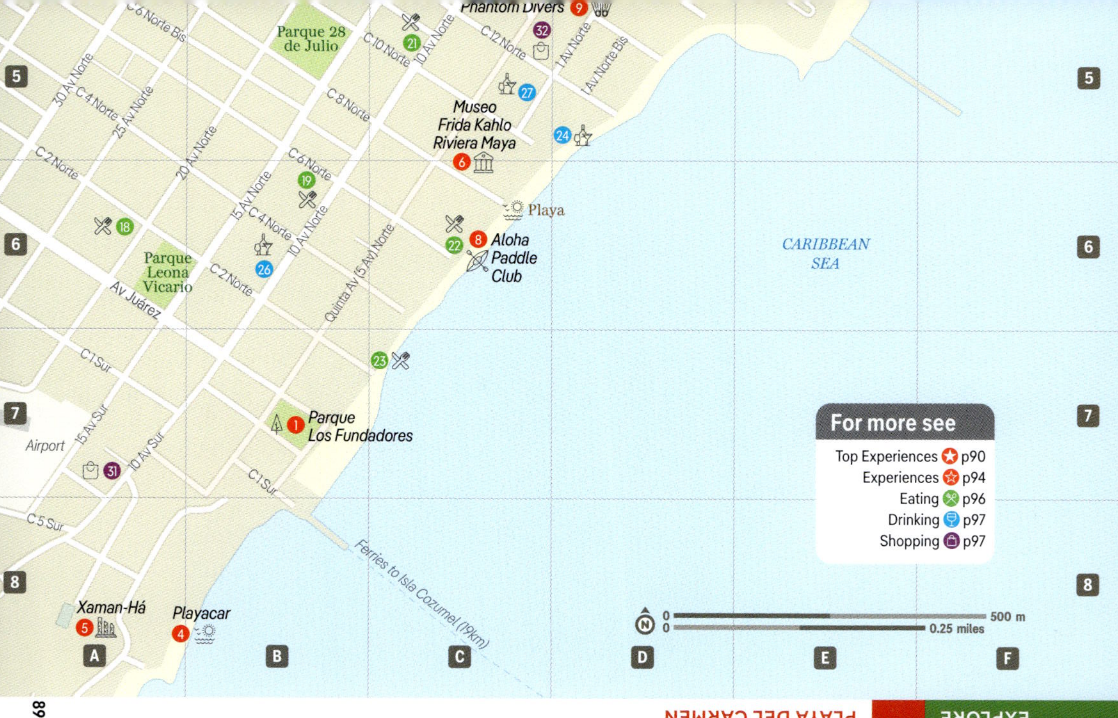
Phantom Divers
9
32
21
Parque 28
de Julio
C 6 Norte Bis
C 10 Norte
10 Av Norte
C 12 Norte
1 Av Norte
1 Av Norte Bis
30 Av Norte
C 4 Norte
25 Av Norte
C 8 Norte
27
Museo
Frida Kahlo
Riviera Maya
6
24
C 2 Norte
20 Av Norte
C 6 Norte
19
15 Av Norte
C 4 Norte
10 Av Norte
Playa
18
22
8
Aloha
Paddle
Club
26
Parque
Leona
Vicario
C 2 Norte
Quinta Av (5 Av) Norte
Av Juárez
CARIBBEAN
SEA
C 1 Sur
23
15 Av Sur
10 Av Sur
1
Parque
Los Fundadores
Airport
31
C 1 Sur
For more see
Top Experiences p90
Experiences p94
Eating p96
Drinking p97
Shopping p97
C 5 Sur
Ferries to Isla Cozumel (19km)
Xaman-Há
5
Playacar
4
0
500 m
0
0.25 miles
A
B
C
D
E
F
5
6
7
8

★ TOP EXPERIENCE

Riviera Maya's Cenotes

It's easy to see why the Maya thought cenotes – fathomless cerulean pools, dancing shafts of light, jungle-clad settings or stalactite-filled caverns – were sacred entrances to the underworld. Thousands of cenotes dot the peninsula, and they are prime spots for swimming, diving and relaxing in nature.

PLANNING TIPS
Visit early (by 10am) to beat the midday crowds. Pack a swimsuit, towel and water shoes or sandals, but don't put on sunscreen because it pollutes the waters. Typically, admission costs M$300 to M$600 (often cash only), and opening hours run 8am to 5pm.

Parque Dos Ojos

With several impressive cenotes, **Dos Ojos** offers guided snorkeling tours of amazing underwater caverns, where you float past illuminated stalactites and stalagmites in an eerie wonderland. The price is higher than most, but you could spend a hours at this expansive site. It's also handy to have a car, as it's around 3km from the highway.

You'll need to book cave dives with off-site outfitters such as **Phantom Divers** (p95) in Playa del Carmen or **La Calypso** (p115) in Tulum.

Cenote Cristalino

Around 23km south of Playa del Carmen, just off the highway, small **Cenote Cristalino** lives up to its name with crystal-clear waters surrounded by dense green forest. The cenote has a small cliff where you can launch yourself into the water.

Cenote Azul

Conveniently by the main highway, **Cenote Azul** (pictured) is one of the easiest Riviera Maya cenotes to visit. It's also one of the region's most beautiful natural attractions. Leap off the small cliff into the clear waters at the cenote's deep end, or spend the day snorkeling among the rocks on the shallow side.

FILIPPO CARLOT/SHUTTERSTOCK

Ruta de los Cenotes

Some 35km northeast of Playa del Carmen is the turnoff to **Ruta de los Cenotes**, a jungle-lined road passing over a dozen enchanting swimming spots. You'll need a car to properly explore the area. Start at **Siete Bocas**, which has both a subterranean area and an open-air cenote that you can leap into from small cliffs. Some 10km west, **La Noria** is a mostly closed (cavern-like) cenote with stalactites, and you can pay extra for zip-lining or horseback rides. Nearby, you could spend a half day at **Zapote Ecopark**, with four different cenotes (two open, two closed), plus add-ons like aquatic zip-lines.

QUICK BREAK

If you're heading to Yal-Kú or the Ruta de los Cenotes, stop off in Akumal, a charming town with some lovely restaurants, including seaside **La Buena Vida**.

Walk Playa del Carmen

A wander through the heart of this seaside city takes you past photogenic plazas, little-known galleries and hidden artwork, with ample opportunities to shop and snack along the way. Come in the morning to see the city at its most peaceful, or late in the day when there's music in the air and palpable energy on the streets.

START	END	LENGTH
Parque Los Fundadores	Palacio Municipal	1km; 1 hour

1 Plaza of Activities

Anchoring the southern end of Quinta Avenida is **Parque Los Fundadores**, a tree-fringed square where you can take the pulse of the city. Snack stands dole out coconut waters and fresh fruit, while tourists line up for photos beside the giant 'Playa del Carmen' sign and buskers show off their musical skills or even high-flying abilities.

2 Sculptural Backdrop

Anchoring the seaside end of Parque Los Fundadores is a massive sculpture known as the **Portal Maya**. Its swirling figures pay homage to the coast's quintessential elements: water (left side) and wind (right), while the hoops evoke that pre-Colombian game of *juego de pelota*.

3 Photogenic Chapel

As you leave the park, take a peek inside the **Capilla de Nuestra Señora del Carmen**, a colonial-style white chapel dedicated to the patron saint of fishers. It was built in the 1960s when the settlement was home to about 300 people (most seafarers), compared to the 300,000-plus residents today.

4 Vertiginous Heart of Playa

Turn right along pedestrianized **Quinta Avenida** and take in the scene. The next few blocks are packed with open-sided restaurants, where live salsa and rock spills onto the terraces in the evening. You may also stumble upon other freelance performers, from breakdancers to twirling folkloric groups.

5 The Gallery Scene

Just past Calle 6, keep an eye out for the narrow lane leading to **Gastón Charó Gallery**, which showcases the paintings, sculptures, photography and jewelry of more than 40 Mexican and international artists. You'll also see works by the founder's namesake, including some surrealist sculptures.

6 Public Gathering Space

Turn left up Calle 8 to see the dreamlike *Equilibrio* mural by Mexican artist Senkoe. Two blocks up, you'll reach **Plaza 28 de Julio**. Locals come for periodic concerts, big markets and seasonal events (including colorful displays around Día de Muertos and Christmas). There's also a small playground for those traveling with kids.

7 Playa's Grand Mural

Overlooking the plaza is the low-rise **Palacio Municipal** (Town Hall). Say hello to the guards, then wander into the courtyard, where you'll see a huge (29m x 9m) mural depicting key elements of Maya history and mythology as well as iconic Playa monuments, including the **Xaman-Há ruins**, the Capilla de Nuestra Señora del Carmen and the Palacio Municipal itself.

EXPERIENCES

Join the Action on Playa's Central Beachfront
WATERFRONT

MAP: 1 P88 B7

One of Playa's most vibrant destinations lies along the golden shores just north of **Parque Los Fundadores**. The 500m stretch from here to Zenzi Beach (p97) restaurant is a playground of seafront dining and drinking, lounge chairs for hire and all manner of action on and off the water – from sandcastle building and frolicking in the waves, to paddle ball and shell hunting along the shore.

Watch the Sunrise from Playa 88
BEACH

MAP: 2 P88 F1

The crowds start to thin as you go north of Muelle Constituyentes, and at **Playa 88** you'll reach a gorgeous expanse of sparsely developed beachfront. Backed by palms and coastal scrub, the sands are wider and cleaner (earning the beach Blue Flag status) and it's an ideal spot for watching the sunrise. Access it along Calle 88.

Escape the Crowds at Punta Esmeralda
BEACH

MAP: 3 P88 F1

From Playa 88, keep strolling 1km north to **Punta Esmeralda**. Set on the city's northern edge, this scenic spot (another Blue Flag beach) has soft white sand and ample room to run about. There's a small natural pool, which makes a fine spot for kids (or adults) to splash about. If you're eager to head straight to Punta Esmeralda, it's about 4km from the center of Quinta Avenida, making for a pleasant bike ride.

Walk the Family-Friendly Seaside of Playacar
BEACH

MAP: 4 P88 A8

South of Centro, you'll find some enchanting coastal spots. Just beyond the ferry terminal (south of Parque Fundadores), kick off your shoes and walk along the well-kept sands of **Playacar**. Backed by beachfront condos and all-inclusive resorts, this beach feels exclusive, but it's open to all as long as you arrive along the shoreline. The inviting sands and shallow waters are ideal for families, without the music-blaring beach clubs further north.

Photograph Maya Ruins
ARCHAEOLOGICAL SITE

MAP: 5 P88 A8

Just off Playacar (a few minutes' walk from the ferry terminal), you'll see a small turnoff to the ruins of **Xaman-Há** *(free)*. Though there's no signage at the site, the atmospheric remains are well worth a visit as you'll likely have them all to yourself. Xaman-Há, which means 'northern water,' likely dates from the mid-13th century. Nearly swallowed by the surrounding trees, the low-rise structures were once a key departure point for Maya pilgrims to the island of Cozumel, home to a temple dedicated to Ixchel, the goddess of fertility and the moon.

Learn About the Life of Frida Kahlo

MUSEUM

MAP: 6 P88 **C6**

The admission is pricey, and there are no original works by the famous painter on display, but the small **Museo Frida Kahlo Riviera Maya** *(adult/child M$350/90)* does an excellent job bringing Kahlo to life. Knowledgeable guides take you through pivotal moments, with the assistance of artwork by other Mexican artists (including from Playa del Carmen). A short animated film captures the trauma of the accident that forever marked her, and a model of her recovery bed features fantastical images flickering across mirror-like butterflies. Elsewhere, peek through tiny holes at miniaturized scenes from Kahlo's life.

Immerse Yourself in the World of Chocolate

MUSEUM

MAP: 7 P88 **C3**

Choco-Story *(choco-storymexico.com; adult/child M$210/110)* is a journey through the history of chocolate. Seven thematic rooms show different facets of this beloved foodstuff, from its role in commerce and ceremonies during the days of the ancient Maya to the drawing rooms of 18th-century European royals. Each room is set with a different scene (one depicts a rather grisly sacrifice), as well as replicas of fascinating archeological finds (like a 5500-year-old cacao-shaped mortar likely used to prepare hallucinogenic drinks that were discovered in Ecuador). Press a button in each room for audio commentary (available in English and five other languages). The experience ends in a small, modern production room, where you can taste the raw and finished forms, including milk chocolate, dark chocolate and white chocolate. The gift shop sells plenty of chocolaty decadence, including nicely spiced bars with some chili.

BEST ACTIVITIES

Aloha Paddle Club

MAP: 8 P88 **C6**

Take a sunrise SUP tour from the beach, or rent your own board to explore the shore independently. Based out of Fusion (p97).

Phantom Divers

MAP: 9 P88 **D5**

A pioneer of diving with bull sharks (the season runs from November to March), it has a solid reputation for two-tank dive excursions. Cenote dives are also possible.

Dani Sailing

MAP: 10 P88 **F3**

Take a two-hour catamaran trip, which includes a stop for snorkeling, or book a parasailing adventure. Find it at Mamita's Beach Club.

LISTINGS

Best Places for...

$ Budget $$ Midrange $$$ Top End

Eating

Cafes & Breakfast Spots

Chez Céline $$
11 E2
Good, healthy breakfasts and perfectly flaky baked goods are what keep this French-run bakery-cafe busy. *7:30am-11:30pm*

Choux Choux Cafe $$
12 C3
Inviting, rustic-chic setting for tartines, eggs Benedict, baguette sandwiches and fanciful coffees and smoothies. *7am-5:30pm Mon-Sat, to 2:30pm Sun*

Francesca $$
13 E1
Tuck into tasty baked goods, omelets, frothy lattes and vitamin-rich juice combos at this Italian-run bakery. *7:30am-10:30pm Mon-Sat, to 2:30pm Sun*

Ah Cacao $$

E3
This small Playa chain with four locations (all on Quinta Avenida) has many fans of its mochas, hot chocolates and desserts. *7:15am-11:15pm*

Garden Restaurants

La Cueva del Chango $$$

F2
Known for its fresh and natural ingredients, 'the monkey's cave' has seating in a jungly *palapa* (thatched-roof structure) setting or a verdant garden. *8am-10pm Mon-Sat, to 2pm Sun*

La Perla Pixán $$$

F2
Another enchanting outdoor eatery on Calle 38, with outstanding dishes from the Yucatán, Oaxaca and beyond. *8am-midnight*

Affordable Eats

El Fogón $

C3
This colorful, convivial and very casual spot is a local favorite for tacos of juicy perfection, especially tacos *al pastor* (marinated pork). *1pm-midnight*

Asadero El Pollo $

A6
Follow the scent of chargrilled cooking at this unfussy spot, where locals line up for smoky chicken (half or whole) served with rice, salsas and tortillas. *10am-6pm*

International Flavors

Falafel Nessya $
19 B6
A tiny eatery a few blocks inland serving outstanding and filling falafel sandwiches or platters (with hummus and fries). *noon-11pm*

Kobma $$

D4
Atmospheric spot for pan-Asian cooking, including Thai curries, pork-belly ramen, veggie spring rolls and sushi. *4-11pm*

La Famiglia $$

C5
Superb wood-fired pizza and handmade pasta, ravioli and gnocchi. Playa is a magnet for Italian res-

taurants, but La Famiglia ranks among the best of them. *11am-11pm*

Beachfront Dining

Fusion $$

22 C6

Perfectly located beach bar and restaurant facing the sea with a good mix of seafood, Mexican classics and pub fare. *9am-6pm*

La Tarraya $$

 C7

One of Playa's oldest restaurants serves up satisfying, reasonably priced seafood overlooking the sands (near Calle 2 Norte). *noon-8pm*

Drinking

Live Music

Zenzi Beach

24 D5

This seaside beach club and restaurant is a great place to sip cocktails on the sand, and there's live music most nights. *9am-1am*

La Bodeguita del Medio

 E2

An icon on Quinta Avenida, this Cuban restaurant-bar stages live Cuban jazz or salsa most nights. *noon-1:30am*

Cocktails

El Tigre

26 B6

An upscale twist on the Mexican cantina, with a vintage-chic interior and tasty snacks to go with the cocktails. *3-11pm*

Dirty Martini

 C5

A favorite expat drinking den, with a friendly crowd and perfect martinis (two-for-one on Tuesdays). *3pm-2am*

Craft Beer

Chela de Playa

 F2

Grab a spot on the leafy terrace and order a sampler of quality drafts from this Playa de Carmen microbrewer. *noon-midnight*

Club de la Cerveza

 E2

Right on Quinta Avenida is this much-loved spot for outstanding beers (including rotating drafts) you won't find elsewhere. *4pm-1am*

Colectivo Mexicano Cervecero

30 F1

Gastropub with a focus on regional craft beers, which pair nicely with the fish or shrimp tacos. *4pm-1am*

Shopping

Handicrafts & Textiles

Guerrero Corazón

31 A7

Just off the beaten path, this inviting shop celebrates Guerrero's craft-making traditions with jewelry, toys, bags made of natural fibers, fragrances and skincare products. *9am-7pm*

Rosalia Textiles Mayas

32 C5

On Quinta Avenida, this huge, open-sided shop has woven blankets, tablecloths, embroidered dresses and blouses, and other items made by artisans from Chiapas. *8am-1am*

Hamacamarte

33 E2

A small shop on lush Calle 38 with a good selection of colorful, handmade hammocks, as well as pillowcases, placemats, satchels, cutting boards and other craft items. *9am-9pm*

★ WORTH A TRIP

Bacalar

Bacalar is a captivating little town overlooking a picturesque lagoon in the far south of the peninsula. Spend the day boating, kayaking or swimming, followed by dinner and drinks at a waterfront restaurant, or join locals on the main square (with food stalls, music and craft vendors).

PLANNING TIP
Reach Bacalar by train or bus. The Tren Maya station is 5km from the center (taxis charge M$50), while the 1st-class ADO bus station is 2km north of the Plaza Principal.

Boat Tours

The most popular outing in Bacalar is a boat tour out to some of the most scenic parts of the lagoon. Numerous agencies, including DayTour Bacalar (operating out of **Casa China**), offer excursions. These take you to the Black Cenote (the lake's deepest part), the Pirates' Channel for a swim and the Isla de los Pájaros for more swimming and the chance to spot birds. A three-hour tour costs around M$450 by pontoon boat and M$800 by sailboat. Afterward, you're welcome to borrow *(free)* kayaks to paddle around the lagoon or climb up a lighthouse-like tower for a view over the water.

Paddling Adventures

When the wind is low, the lagoon is a great spot for exploring on your own by kayak or SUP. If the sun's beating down, find a shallow spot and go for a swim. Just be sure to mind the roped-off protected zones (around Bird Island, for instance). Many lake-front guesthouses rent gear (available to nonguests, too), including **Yak Lake House**. There are also sunrise paddle tours, which can be an enchanting way to start the day.

GUAJILLO STUDIO/SHUTTERSTOCK

Bacalar's Fortress

A few steps from the Plaza Principal, the imposing **Fuerte de San Felipe** (*M$110*; pictured) is a fascinating 18th-century relic. The thick stone walls bristle with cannons, and you only need to imagine water in the now-dry moat to realize the difficulty of breaching it. One thick-walled building houses a small, worthwhile museum with pottery and carvings (including an unusual phallic bird) from precolonial civilizations, muskets and an astrolabe commonly used by sailors, and model ships. The fortress keeps long hours (10am to 7pm Tuesday to Sunday), making it a fine spot for around sunset when the sky (sometimes) takes on auburn hues.

TAKE A BREAK
There are lots of good restaurants in Bacalar, but **La Playita** is a standout for its expansive tropical garden and waterfront setting, and you can swim right off the dock.

Boardwalk Stroll

On the lagoon, less than 1km north of the fort, you'll find the entrance to the **Balneario Ecológico**

CYCLING TOUR
Pro Seal runs one-of-a-kind bicycling tours out to Maya communities, with forest stops and wildlife-watching opportunities along the way. Contact via WhatsApp *(+52 983 156 5413)*.

(M$20). This boardwalk path heads out past mangroves and tiny stromatolites (the sand-colored, rocklike formations in the water on your left) and over the water, a quadrangle totaling some 400m. You can go for a swim, as many locals do, or look for small crocodilians amid the greenery close to shore. This is also a good spot for spying great blue herons, great egrets and other avian life, particularly late in the afternoon.

Waterside Relaxing

If the swimming spots in the center of town feel too crowded, head to **Cocalitos** *(adult/child M$100/50)* for a more laid-back experience. The water is shallow, there are stromatolites to admire and a grassy lawn for stretching out. There's no

SAILINGSTONE TRAVEL/SHUTTERSTOCK

restaurant or bar, though you're welcome to bring your own drinks and snacks. It's an easy 4.5km south of the center, just before rounding the bend to Cenote Azul.

Floating the 'Rapids'

A unique way to experience the allure of Bacalar is to float down **Los Rápidos** (*rapidosdebacalar.com; adult/child M$200/150*; pictured), a narrow part of the lagoon that's dotted with stromatolites. After paying admission, take the walkway to the right for 400m and then hop in the water and float back to your starting point. There's a waterfront restaurant, plus **kayaks for hire** *(single/double per hour M$200/400)*. Los Rápidos are 14km south of the center, about a 20-minute drive. Taxis charge M$200 each way.

Evenings on the Plaza

When the sun sets and the grackles take up their evening song (at times a roar) in **Plaza Principal**, Bacalar can feel like an enchanted corner of the Yucatán. Couples stroll beneath the lights strung through the trees. Food vendors spread a smorgasbord of temptations: Argentine empanadas (and roast meat sandwiches), Oaxacan *tlayudas* (a large crispy tortilla topped with various goodies), *marquesitas* (waffle-like crepes), *elote* (corn on the cob), churros and smoothies. You'll also find a wide mix of craft vendors – it's a good place to support local talent.

Cenote Azul

Ringed by dense forest and hidden just inland from the lagoon, **Cenote Azul** *(M$100)* is a delightful spot for a swim in waters that reach 90m deep (life jackets provided); there's also a simple restaurant. The cenote is about 5km south of the center, and is a pleasant bike ride along the main road.

ARTISTS OF BACALAR

Boasting two locations in town, the Colectivo de Artistas en Bacalar (aka **CAB**) is a collective with unique pottery, paintings and streetwear made by local artists. Find it at @cab_colectivo.

LIVE MUSIC

One of the liveliest spots near the waterfront, **La Catrina** is a bar-eatery that draws dance lovers for the live salsa or *cumbia* on weekends.

See p118
for eating,
drinking and
shopping
listings

Explore Tulum

Tulum's spectacular coastline, with its confectioner-sugar sands, cobalt water and balmy breezes, makes it one of the top beach destinations in Mexico. Adding to the allure are some impressive Maya ruins perched above the shores that are now part of the huge new nature reserve of Parque del Jaguar. There's also excellent snorkeling and diving, enticing cenotes (limestone sinkholes) nearby and buzzing nightlife on and off the shore. Tulum has two distinct personalities: the upscale beach clubs of the Zona Hotelera aim for glitz and glamour, while the bustling town center sometimes feels more like a truck stop than a tropical paradise.

Getting Around

Bus

The centrally located ADO bus terminal is on Avenida Tulum. There's also a bus service from here to the Tren Maya rail station.

Colectivo

Colectivos (small buses) pass frequently along Avenida Tulum for Parque del Jaguar and Playa del Carmen. *Colectivos* to the beach leave from the corner of Venus Oriente and Orion Sur.

Bicycle

Bicycles are a good way to travel the 5km between the town and the beach. Rental outfits include iBike Tulum and CicloBike *(M$150 to M$200 per day)*.

THE BEST

MAYA RUINS El Castillo (p106)

BEACH Playa Pescadores (p109)

NATURE RESERVE Sian Ka'an (p115)

SNORKELING Laguna Yal-Kú (p116)

COCKTAILS Batey (p115)

Sian Ka'an Biosphere Reserve (p115)
SAILINGSTONE TRAVEL/SHUTTERSTOCK

A B C D E F
1 2 3 4
0 2 km
0 1 mile
Av Cobá
16
MEX 109
17 18 19 20 21
MEX 307
C Okot
Av Tulum
Av Kukulkán
TULUM
See Enlargement
Muyil
40
26
22
28
7 Sur
1 Poniente
Carretera Tulum-Boca Paila
34
Av Cobá
15
Av Chechen
21 Poniente
Parque del Jaguar
Carretera Bocapaila
Playa Pescadores
Playa Mangle
For more see
Top Experiences p106
Experiences p114
Eating p118
Drinking p119
Shopping p119

CARIBBEAN SEA
12 Papaya Playa Project
1 Playa Punta Piedra
2 La Eufemia
4 Ziggy's
9 Kapen-Ha
41
35
6 Delek
3 Sana Sana Cafe
5 Akiin
31
7 Sian Kite Tulum
13
38
15
33 Poniente
39 Poniente
Av Kukulkán
Av 65 Sur
Carretera Tulum-Boca Paila
TULUM
8 La Calypso
15 Mexico Kan Tours
10 Batey
11 La Guarida
14 Community Tours Sian Ka'an
Main Plaza
4 Oriente
2 Poniente
Orión Norte
Beta Norte
Osiris Norte
Alfa Norte
Centauro Norte
Satélite Norte
Géminis Norte
Sagitario Poniente
Polar Poniente
Av Tulum
Andromeda Oriente
Alfa Sur
Osiris Sur
Beta Sur
Orión Sur
Centauro Sur
Satélite Sur
Sol Oriente
Venus Oriente
0 200 m
0 0.1 miles
A B C D E F
5 6 7 8

★ TOP EXPERIENCE

Parque del Jaguar

Years in the making, the Parque del Jaguar, which opened in 2025, encompasses protected beaches, lookout towers, forest trails and a museum full of Maya artifacts. The big draw is the archaeological zone (aka Tulum Ruins), with its collection of temples and pre-Hispanic monuments, along with stunning vistas over the Caribbean.

MAP P104 **D2**

PLANNING TIP
Make a full day of it, visiting the ruins at opening time (before the crowds arrive) and then explore the rest of Parque del Jaguar before enjoying some beach time. Admission is M$350 (M$450 including the ruins). Open for beach access 8am-6pm, museum and ruins 9am-3:30pm.

El Castillo

Standing nearly 8m high near the cliff face, this imposing structure once served as a lighthouse that guided Maya ships to port. In the upper level, note the small windows, which would blaze with light when fires were lit in the evening. The watchtower was appropriately named **El Castillo** (The Castle) by the Spaniards. Note the Toltec-style Kukulcánes (plumed serpents) at the corners, echoing those at Chichén Itzá.

Templo del Dios Descendente

This **temple** gets its name from a relief figure of a Descending God depicted in a niche above the building's door. The figure's legs are splayed, with his arms below and his face appearing beneath a headdress. His hands are holding an unknown object. Note the slightly off-kilter slope of the walls and door, which was created intentionally by Maya builders.

Casa del Cenote

Named for the small sinkhole at its southern base, the **Casa del Cenote** was built atop a vital water source for the city. Peer inside and down into the depths and you might catch a glimpse of little silvery fish as they turn sideways in the murky water. A small tomb was found in the *casa*.

Templo de las Pinturas

With its columns, carvings and two-story construction, the **Temple of the Frescoes** was among the most elaborate at Tulum. The facade on the lower temple has relief masks and sculptures, with colored murals on an inner wall. The murals have been partially restored but are nearly impossible to make out. This monument might have been the last built by the Maya before the Spanish conquest.

Templo del Dios del Viento

All on its own on a high point overlooking the sea, this two-level **structure** is unusual for its

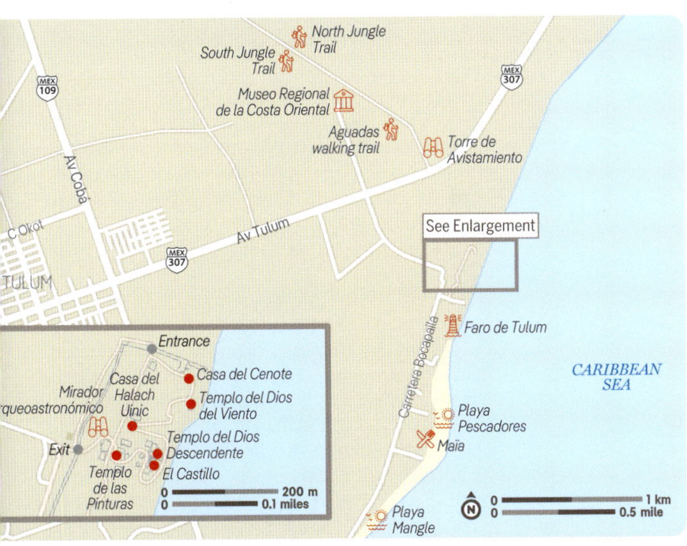

WALKABOUT PHOTO GUIDES/SHUTTERSTOCK

round base, which is associated with Kukulcán, the plumed serpents of the Maya god of the wind. There's a small altar within and evidence that the building had a ceremonial use until the early 1900s. According to legend, when a whistling sound emitted from the building's upper story, Maya knew to take shelter for approaching storms and hurricanes.

Casa del Halach Uinic

A short walk from the Templo de las Pinturas, the **House of the Halach Uinic** (pictured) is named after the royal lord (and high priest) who likely lived here. Though part of the sizable building is in ruins, you can still make out the staircase leading up to the column-lined entrance and a stucco image above the portal just beyond. It's another recurring image of the Descending God, which may relate to Ah Muzen Cab, the revered god of the bees.

Mirador Arqueoastronómico

Not marked on most maps is a fantastic **viewpoint** overlooking the ruins. Get there by turning right after passing the Temple of the Frescoes and heading west (inland) to an open expanse where you'll have a sweeping view over El Castillo and the surrounding temples. A small sign points out the perfect alignment of the buildings in relation to solstices and equinoxes. At sunrise during the winter solstice, sun beams stream through an opening in the top of the Temple of the Descending God.

QUICK BREAK
Have breakfast, lunch or drinks at a beach-facing restaurant near Playa Pescadores. **Maïa** has a sizable menu of bowls, salads, enchiladas and sharing plates, with vegetarian options.

Beaches

Parque del Jaguar protects some lovely stretches of sand. Around 300m past the ruins, you'll reach the **Faro de Tulum**, a reconstruction of an ancient lighthouse. There's a nice view over the shore and a path down to the beach. Once on the sand, you can stroll 1.5km south, where you'll reach **Playa Mangle**, with a rocky shoreline farther along. There are other access points to the shore, including popular **Playa Pescadores** (pictured on p110), where several restaurants dole out seafood and drinks, and rent out loungers and sunshades for prime sea gazing. Boat captains lead **tours** *(60/90-minute tour about M$300/500)* from the beach throughout the day, which take in views of the ruins followed by a snorkeling stop.

Museum

The small **Museo Regional de la Costa Oriental** has two sunlit rooms of artifacts, where you can spend a half-hour or so learning about the Maya. A mix of original pieces and reproductions shed light on mythology, cultural practices (human sacrifices, burial traditions, ball games), astronomy and the Maya calendar. Among the displays are fine stone carvings, jade jewelry and architectural masks.

LOES KIEBOOM/SHUTTERSTOCK

Observation Tower

About 800m from the museum, the **Torre de Avistamiento** (Observation Tower) offers intriguing views from a circular open-topped deck some 10m above the ground. Various panels, in English and Spanish, point out Maya navigational strategies, unique architectural elements and insight into the region's plant and animal life.

Walking Trails

Between the Torre de Avistamiento and the museum, you'll find the 700m **Aguadas walking trail**, which heads through forest to a small section of wetlands. North of the museum are other spots for a walk: the 1.4km **South Jungle Trail** and the 950m **North Jungle Trail**. Mornings offer the best chance to see a variety of birds, such as social flycatchers, tropical kingbirds and great kiskadees.

★ TOP EXPERIENCE

Muyil

First inhabited in 300 BCE, Muyil was the biggest and most important Maya settlement inside present-day Sian Ka'an Biosphere Reserve. Visit ruins *(M$80)*, take a forest walk and go for a boating and swimming excursion *(M$1000)*.

MAP P104 **A3**

Ruins

Near the entrance, **Structure 7H-3** contains visible fragments of mural painting, as well as Maya west coast–style features like vaulted ceilings and column-supported lintels. Follow the short trail from there to reach 17m **El Castillo** (aka Structure 8I-13), Muyil's most impressive building.

Forest Walk & Lookout Tower

After seeing the ruins, follow the 500m path through the forest. Come early morning or late afternoon for the best chance to see wildlife. About halfway along the path, you can climb a wooden **lookout tower** for views over the jungle and the lagoons to the east.

Boating & Swimming

At the waterfront, boats can whisk you across Laguna de Muyil and through a narrow canal into Laguna Chunyaxché. Docking on the edge of another canal, you can plunge into the water, the highlight of a trip to Muyil. Comfortably wrapped in a life vest, you'll float along crystalline waters, past mangrove trees arching into the water, with twittering birds hidden in the branches.

Bring a mask and snorkel to see fish along the way. It takes no effort, as the current takes you along the 800m journey – relax and enjoy the ride.

PLANNING TIP
Colectivos make the 25-minute trip to Muyil hourly (on the hour) from a stop about one block west of the Tulum bus station on the main road, Avenida Tulum.

Walk Tulum

While most people come for the beach, Tulum Town (aka Tulum Pueblo) is a fascinating place to browse for wood carvings, ceramics, jewelry and other handicrafts. Dusty Avenida Tulum may not look like Madison Ave, but you'll find a trove of artisan stores and snack stops. Visit in the late afternoon to beat the heat.

START	END	LENGTH
Bendita Tierra	Mixik	1km; 1½ hours

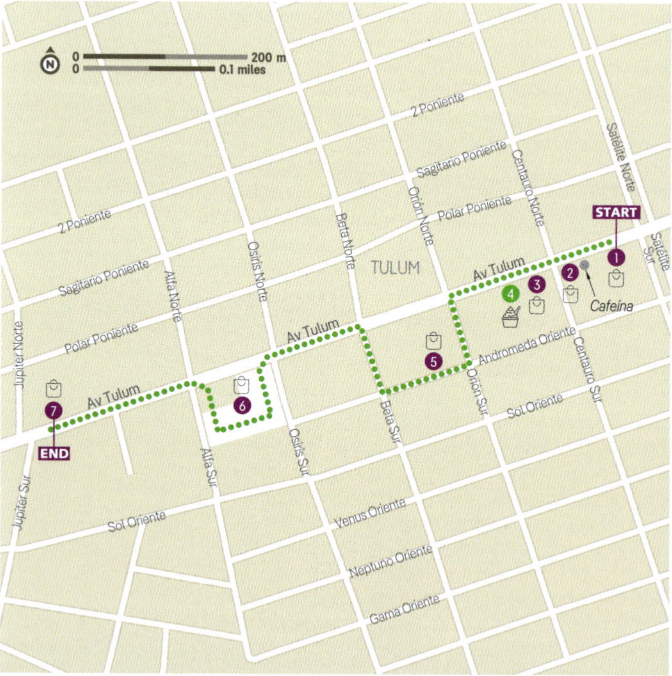

1 Artisans of Tulum & Beyond

The tiny shop **Bendita Tierra** features 15 artisans' work, including *barro negro* (black pottery), tin hearts from San Miguel de Allende, fabric-covered notebooks and whimsical Frida Kahlo–inspired paintings. Owner Elena Gonzalez Izquierdo is often on hand and can give insight into the makers behind the crafts.

2 Pottery & Souvenirs

Turn left out of the shop and pick up a coffee a few doors down at Cafeína, if you need a pick-me-up. Otherwise continue to **Casa Hernández** on the corner, where you'll find lots of eye-catching souvenirs, including colorfully painted Talavera pottery, textiles, amber jewelry and delightfully kitschy Frida Kahlo–inspired artwork. The prices are fair.

3 Tulum Designs

Cross Calle Centauro Sur and you'll soon reach **Tribalik**, a small boutique specializing in apparel with an effortless Tulum style. High-quality cotton or linen fabric feature jungle-print motifs or solid earth tones on dresses, blouses and men's collared shirts. You'll also find fedora-like hats, chunky jewelry and upcycled notebooks.

4 Heavenly Gelato

Keep going along Avenida Tulum and you'll pass **Panna e Cioccolato**. This tiny snack spot (with two locations in town) was proudly born in the Riviera Maya and features a rotating lineup of more than a dozen rich flavors (try spicy chocolate or tropical flavors like passionfruit or guava with cheese).

5 Vintage Style

Head around the corner and turn right to arrive at **Honesta Vintage**. Tulum's best secondhand store has apparel from decades past as well as upcycled designs – vintage fabrics turned into modern tops and boots featuring repurposed denim. The store has Hawaiian shirts, leather jackets and eye-catching hats.

6 A Vibrant Plaza

Back on Avenida Tulum, walk two blocks to the main plaza, **Parque dos Aguas**, a favorite local gathering space, especially in the evenings. From about 4:30pm until after 10pm, you'll find vendors selling crafts (shell bracelets and the like) and food carts plying *marquesitas* (waffle-like crepes), *elote* (corn on the cob), churros and other temptations.

7 One-of-a-Kind Crafts

Another block down, **Mixik** is a colorful store packed with folk art and crafts. Tiny boxes feature whimsical scenes of skeletons dancing, playing music or sitting in jail, and there are also wall hangings, embroidered dresses, leather bags, jewelry and glassware.

EXPERIENCES

Find Your Slice of Tropical Paradise

BEACH

MAP: 1 P104 **C6**

With palm-backed beaches overlooking cerulean seas, Tulum doesn't lack for pretty shoreline. Some 10km of sublime white sands lie between Tulum's archaeological zone and the Sian Ka'an Biosphere Reserve fronting the Caribbean, which is clear and temperate almost year-round. From the main road through town, Avenida Cobá (Hwy 15) leads down to the shore. At the roundabout, heading left leads to the protected beaches of the Parque del Jaguar (p106). Going right leads to the Zona Hotelera, a narrow, busy road backed by shoreline hotels, beach clubs and restaurants.

Around 1.7km south of the roundabout is **Playa Punta Piedra**. This free public beach is an easy access point if you don't want to hassle with the beach clubs farther south. A small rocky outcrop offers views over the shore.

Enjoy Seaside Relaxing & Dining

BEACH CLUBS

Tulum's prettiest stretch of shoreline begins 1km south of Playa Punta Piedra, though you won't be able to see much from the road. You have a few options to reach the beach: commit to a beach club (with entry fees ranging from US$30 to US$50 or more, which you can put towards food and drink) or simply head to a beachfront restaurant like **La Eufemia** (MAP: 2 P104 **C6**) or **Sana Sana Cafe** (MAP: 3 P104 **B8**). If you're just dining, you won't have access to deck chairs and loungers, but once on the sands, you can explore at your leisure. A few favorite beach clubs are **Ziggy's** (MAP: 4 P104 **B7**; *ziggybeachtulum.com*), which has a laid-back atmosphere, good food and hammocks and beach beds for relaxing. A party-centric vibe pervades **Akiin** (MAP: 5 P104 **B8**; *akiinbeachclubtulum.com*) with its well-placed beach beds backed by palm trees and a small inviting pool. Appealing, unpretentious **Delek** (MAP: 6 P104 **B8**; *delektulum.com*) has relaxing lounge chairs and a low minimum spend.

Swim in a Hidden Cenote

CENOTE

MAP: 9 P104 **B7**

When you need a break from the beach, visit **Kapen-Ha**, a small forest-ringed cenote reached by a boardwalk path through mangroves. Find it behind a small shopping complex (and beside the Casa Teka hotel). There's generally no admission fee, but it's polite to order something from the on-site restaurant.

Sip Tulum's Best Mojitos

BAR

MAP: 10 P104 **E7**

Calle Centauro Sur, just off Avenida Tulum, is the epicenter of Tulum's nightlife. Start the night at

Batey, a much-loved expat watering hole with a back garden where bands perform. Don't miss Batey's signature drink: mojitos made with freshly pressed sugarcane.

Catch DJs & Live Performances

BAR

MAP: 11 P104 **E7**

One block from Batey, **La Guarida** makes a great hideaway for an evening of cocktails, snacks and first-rate wines. You'll find various rooms and terraces secreted in the multilevel space, and there are often live performances of funk, soul, flamenco, reggae and other sounds.

Party on the Beach

BAR

MAP: 12 P104 **C5**

Tulum's beach clubs are largely a daytime affair. On weekends, however, you can catch some of its best parties at seaside places like **Papaya Playa Project** *(papayaplayaproject.com)*.

BEST ACTIVITIES

Sian Kite Tulum

MAP: 7 P104 **B8**

Offers kitesurfing and SUP lessons, as well as three-hour SUP tours from a beachside location in Tulum's Zona Hotelera.

La Calypso

MAP: 8 P104 **D7**

This long-running dive center specializes in diving Dos Ojos and other cenotes. You can also sign up for a more traditional reef dive or a snorkeling trip.

Mexico Kan Tours

see 15 **E7**

One of Tulum's top agencies, this pro outfit runs a wide array of excursions, including trips to Sian Ka'an Biosphere Reserve, popular cycling excursions and birdwatching in the jungle.

See Wildlife in Sian Ka'an

NATURE RESERVE

Ten kilometers south of Tulum, an arch over the coastal road marks the entrance to **Sian Ka'an** (MAP: 13 P104 **B8**; Where the Sky is Born), a jungle-clad biosphere reserve with

TULUM BEFORE THE SPANISH

Tulum's pre-Hispanic peak was during the late post-Classic period (1200–1521 CE), when the settlement was an important port town. The Maya sailed up and down this coast, maintaining trading routes all the way down into Belize. When Juan de Grijalva sailed past in 1518, he was amazed by the sight of the walled city, its buildings painted a gleaming red, blue and yellow and a ceremonial fire flaming atop its seaside watchtower. The thick walls surrounding three sides of Tulum (the fourth side being the sea) protected the city during a period of strife between Maya city-states.

marine and shoreline ecosystems and wildlife-watching opportunities. Unfortunately, it's not very rewarding to drive the badly potholed road toward Punta Allen and visit on your own.

Most beaches are private access only, and you need to get on the water to make the most of a trip. Recommended operators such as **Community Tours Sian Ka'an** (MAP: 14 P104 **D8**; *siankaantours.com.mx*), **Mexico Kan Tours** (MAP: 15 P104 **E7**; *mexicokantours.com*) and **Pixan Ka'an** (*siankaantours.org*) run excursions from Tulum, spending the day boating around the bay (looking for dolphins and sea turtles), checking out birdlife in the mangroves and snorkeling the reef, with a stop in the seaside village of Punta Allen for lunch. Full-day trips cost US$160 to US$200.

Go Wildlife Watching & Zip-Lining

COMMUNITY-RUN ECOTOURISM

MAP: 16 P104 **B1**

Some 20km northeast of Cobá, **Punta Laguna** (*puntalagunamx.com*) makes a good side trip when visiting the temples of Cobá, but you'll need your own car. Here, a small Maya community runs an ecotourism project amid the wildlife-filled forests surrounding a sparkling lagoon. Most people come for the adventure package (per person M$1000; cash only), where you'll look for spider monkeys in the forests, take a boat ride across the lagoon and then try a 240m zip-line. Last is a rappelling descent into Cenote Calaveras.

Snorkel with Sea Turtles

NATURE RESERVE

MAP: 17 P104 **E1**

Akumal (Place of the Turtles in Mayan) lives up to its name, with sea turtles feeding in the clear waters just off the palm-backed beach where **Tsúuk Akumal Parque Natural** (*tsuukakumal.com; M$140*) protects a stretch of shoreline.

To access the aquatic reserve beyond the beach, you have to book a guided snorkel tour (from M$800, including snorkel gear). A certified English-speaking guide will swim with you around the marine sanctuary. **Marine Life Akumal** (*instagram.com/marine.lifemx*) and **Akumal Dive Shop** (*akumaldiveshop.com*) are two reputable outfits.

Akumal is 30km north of Tulum, just off the highway to Playa del Carmen. Many agencies in Tulum and Playa del Carmen offer tours, though you can also book through guides near the beach entrance. There's decent dining and snack options in a complex across the street from the reserve entrance.

Join Aquatic Activities at Laguna Yal-Kú

SWIMMING

MAP: 18 P104 **E1**

Akumal is also home to **Yal-Kú** (*yalkupark.com; adult/child M$300/220*), about 2km past

Tsúuk Akumal Parque Natural. Although turtles are sometimes spotted here, this inviting lagoon is better known for its abundance of fish life, and the crystal-clear water allows for prime viewing. You can rent life vests and snorkel gear. At the lagoon (and at Tsúuk Akumal Parque Natural), sunscreen is prohibited, so wear a rash shirt and seek shade when you're not in the water.

Snorkel at Xcacel — BEACH

MAP: 19 P104 **E1**

Around 20km north of Tulum, on the main highway's east side, a small dirt road leads to the arching bay of **Xcacel** *(M$110)*. This picturesque beach offers good snorkeling (bring your own gear). It's also one of Quintana Roo's most important loggerhead and white sea-turtle nesting sites, and the site is managed by a local community. Food, drinks and the use of sunblock are prohibited on the beach (open 10am to 4pm, closed Monday). Water and fruit are allowed.

Spend a Day at Xcaret — AMUSEMENT PARK

MAP: 20 P104 **E1**

Xcaret *(xcaret.com; adult/child US$133/100)* is a popular adventure park, where it's easy to spend an entire activity-filled day swimming in underground rivers; hanging out on the beach and beside natural pools; and visiting an aquarium, butterfly enclosure and aviary. There are also shows with *voladores* ('flying men' performing a dance suspended from a tall pole) and appealing dining options. It's 58km north of Tulum.

Seek Adventure at Xplor — AMUSEMENT PARK

MAP: 21 P104 **E1**

A short hop from Xcaret, **Xplor** *(xplor.travel; adult/child US$150/113)* is an adventure-lover's playground where you can go zip-lining, drive an amphibious ATV through the jungle, paddle beneath stalactites in an underground river, and swim and hike through caverns. A buffet lunch, snacks and drinks are included with admission.

Dive into Another World — CENOTE

MAP: 22 P104 **A3**

The spectacular **Cenote Angelita** is most notable to divers for the unique, curious, even eerie layer of hydrogen sulfide that 'fogs' the water about halfway through the descent. Look up and see sunlight filtering down through ancient submerged tree branches that are wonderfully creepy – like outstretched witches' arms. The dive is deep and should only be done by experienced divers. Make arrangements through a dive center: La Calypso (p115) has an excellent reputation.

LISTINGS

See p104 for map of locations

Best Places for...

$ Budget $$ Midrange $$$ Top End

Eating

Food Carts & Snacks

Asado Argentino $
23 F6
One of several evening food carts near Pemex (off Géminis Norte), this place fires up mouthwatering grilled steak. *5pm-1am*

Tacos y Tortas El Tío $
24 F7
On a street with several other food carts, El Tío serves delicious tacos and other street snacks. *6pm-2am Mon-Sat*

La Reyna de Michoacan $
25 D8
Across the street from Parque Dos Ojos, this snack spot is famed for its wide selection of *paletas* (popsicles). *8am-11pm*

Cafes & Bakeries

Ki'Bok $$
26 A3
Enjoy a chai latte or flat white (plus satisfying breakfast and lunch fare) while relaxing in the garden. *7am-5pm*

La Fournée $$

D7
Buttery croissants, fresh-squeezed orange juice and baguette sandwiches, best enjoyed in the small garden. *7am-3pm Sun-Fri*

Ma Cherie $$
28 A3
Beautiful, French-owned cafe in La Valeta with heavenly pastries, tartines, salads, quiches and other brunch and lunch fare. *9:30am-3pm*

Seafood

La Negra Tomasa $$

E8
Go early to beat the crowds at this festive, garden-like spot that specializes in seafood-centric tacos, tostadas and sharing plates. *noon-11pm*

La Gloria de Don Pepe $$
see 11 E7
One of Tulum Town's most romantic spots serves up outstanding seafood paella and beautifully presented Spanish tapas. *2:30-10:30pm Tue-Sun*

Sabor de Mar $$

F6
Linger over *torres* (seafood 'towers' piled high with shrimp or fish) and house specialties at this unfussy, outdoor Sinaloa-style seafood joint. *noon-10pm*

Hartwood $$$

B8
This celebrated award winner has a daily changing menu featuring sustainably sourced seafood and local produce. *5:30-10pm*

Vegetarian

Raw Love $$

C8
Plant-based cafe with creative dishes served in a lush outdoor setting in the main street. *9am-8pm*

La Hoja Verde $$

D7
Tulum's best vegetarian restaurant draws fans for its menu of coconut milk curry, quinoa risotto and eggplant and jackfruit moussaka. *8am-11pm*

Italian

Casa Sofia $$

C3
Outstanding, authentic Italian cooking (especially

seafood), plus wood-fired pizzas served in an artfully designed courtyard. *8am-11pm*

Checkpoint Ciao $$

35 B7

On the beach road, bite into flavorful salads and delicious Neapolitan-style wood oven pizza. Best followed by creamy pistachio tiramisu. *11am-midnight*

Burgers & Steaks

Bonita $$

36 D8

The lively outdoor space makes a fine setting for juicy burgers (including vegan), fish and chips, mac and cheese, cocktails and craft beers. *3-11pm*

El Asadero $$$

37 E6

Fires up juicy steaks, including a signature *arranchera* (flank steak), as well as seafood, veggie burritos and grilled nopal (cactus paddle). *3-10pm*

Seaside Meals

La Eufemia $

see 2 C6

A favorite local haunt right on the beach with a buzzing atmosphere, delicious tacos and tangy ceviches. *8am-8pm*

Kuu $$$

38 B8

Tulum's best sushi restaurant has a pretty setting on the beach road and a memorable *omakase* (chef tasting menu) experience. *6pm & 8pm Wed-Mon*

Drinking

Outdoor Spaces

Místico Tulum

39 E7

This chill backyard spot boasts DJs, hookahs and specialty cocktails, and hosts memorable party nights. *9am-2am*

Palma Central

40 A2

Convivial outdoor spot with food trucks and live music most Thursdays through Saturdays, and fiery salsa bands (with free lessons at 7pm) on Tuesdays. *5-11pm Thu-Tue*

Nightclubs

Bonbonniere

41 B7

The well-dressed party people head to this DJ-fueled club on the beach road for bottle service and late-night dancing. Cover charge is about M$1000. *10pm-4am Thu-Sun*

Vagalume

see 5 B8

Beach club and restaurant by day, night spot with DJs performing throughout the week. Cover charge from M$605. *noon-1am Tue-Sun*

Shopping

Arts & Crafts

Tuluminart

42 F7

This small gallery sells colorful works by local artists and quality art supplies. *10am-8pm Mon-Sat*

Mexicarte Tulum

43 D7

Handmade crafts – from *huichol* beadwork to Catrina (skeleton) figurines, plus *luchador* (wrestler) masks – all from Mexican artisans. *10am-10pm*

Clothing & Accessories

Tuna Concept Store

44 E7

A nice boutique for discovering new styles: colorfully patterned silk shirts and summery dresses, eye-catching jewelry and handmade soaps, all made locally. *4-10pm Wed-Mon*

Wayan

45 E7

Founded in 1995 in Cancún, Wayan now has branches all across the Caribbean coast, selling attractive apparel and accessories that embody an organic, jungle-meets-the-sea Tulum vibe. *10am-9pm*

★ WORTH A TRIP

Cobá

Unpaved paths wind through the jungle at this ancient Maya site, home to dozens of impressive structures, including a towering pyramid and several ball courts. Afterwards, you can stroll the peaceful town outside the ruins, or head to some nearby cenotes for a refreshing swim.

PLANNING TIP
Arrive before 11am to beat the big crowds. If you don't have a car, Cobá-bound *colectivos* leave from downtown Tulum, just off Av Tulum on Calle Osiris Norte.

Cycling the Ancient Ruins

Given the distances between some temples, the best way to explore the area is by bike. You can rent one just inside the main gate. Before you reach the bicycle concession, turn right to reach the cluster of sites known as the **Grupo Cobá**. Its dozens of structures include courtyards, vaulted rooms and a *juego de pelota* (ball) court. The biggest structure is La Iglesia (The Church), a towering pyramid that reminded early explorers of a massive medieval cathedral, hence the name.

Pick up a bike and hit the trail to **Grupo Nohoch Mul**, passing several interesting sights along the way. Keep an eye out for the second of Cobá's two *juego de pelota* courts. Look at the ground in the court's center to spot a carved stone skull (the winner or loser of the ball game?) and the carved relief of a jaguar.

Leave time to admire majestic **Nohoch Mul**, a 42m-high temple and the second-tallest pyramid in the Yucatán Peninsula, after Calakmul. Another highlight is the **Grupo de las Pinturas** waintings Group) with its traces of glyphs and frescoes.

Farther out, the buildings of **Grupo Macanxoc** have restored stelae, some of which may depict royal women from Tikal.

Scan this QR code for admission and opening hours.

ARKADIJ SCHELL/SHUTTERSTOCK

Cave Swims near Cobá

Three cenotes *(M$100 each)* lie within reach of Cobá. On hot days, these subterranean water holes make perfect settings for cooling off. If you're not driving, rent a bike in Cobá.

The first of the bunch (6km southwest of Cobá) is **Choo-Ha**, a stalactite-filled cavern with shallow waters ideal for younger children. A short hop from there, **Tankach-Ha** (pictured) is much deeper and has several platforms from which thrill seekers can leap into the water. Head back to the main road and continue another 3km to the remarkably clear waters of **Multum-Ha**.

QUICK BREAK

A short stroll from the ruins' entrance, **Chile Picante** is a two-story thatched-roof restaurant with a huge menu of classics including *cochinita pibil* (Maya-style roasted pork).

See p136
for eating,
drinking and
shopping
listings

Explore Isla Cozumel

Fascinating for its dual personality, Cozumel offers an odd mix of quietly authentic neighborhoods alongside tourist-friendly playgrounds. While diving and snorkeling are the main draws, the easygoing town center is a pleasant place to spend the afternoon, and it's highly gratifying to explore less-visited parts of the island on a rented scooter or a convertible car. The coastal road leads to small Maya ruins, a marine park and cliffside bars, passing captivating scenery along the unforgettable windswept shore. And while the nightlife has nothing on Playa del Carmen or Cancún, there's plenty to do after the sun goes down.

Getting Around

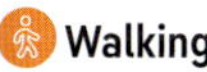

Walking

The main town on the island (San Miguel de Cozumel) is easy to get around on foot. The central plaza is a short stroll from the ferry terminal (where boats run hourly to/from Playa del Carmen).

Car

For DIY exploring, rent a car (from M$1000 per day) and hit the road. Rentadora Isis has old VW convertibles.

Taxi

Agree on a fare before getting in. From town to a beach club runs from M$400 (Mr Sancho's) to M$800 (Punta Sur).

THE BEST

DIVE SITE Santa Rosa Wall (p126)

NATURE RESERVE Punta Sur Eco Beach Park (p132)

BEACH CLUB Mr Sancho's (p134)

SUNSET COCKTAILS Hemingway (p136)

RAINY-DAY ATTRACTION Museo de Cozumel (p132)

Punta Sur Eco Beach Park (p132)
YINGNA CAI/SHUTTERSTOCK

A
B
C
D
E
F
1
2
3
4
0 10 km
0 5 miles
PLAYA DEL CARMEN
CARIBBEAN SEA
Ferry to Playa del Carmen (18km)
Car Ferry to Calica (17km)
Punta Molas
Punta Norte
Laguna Xlapak
Buccanos 9
Av Melgar
Aeropuerto Internacional de Cozumel
25
36
See Enlargement
Miri Adventures 23
SAN MIGUEL DE COZUMEL
Atlantis Submarines 6
Playa la Ceiba
ScubaTony
Blackwater Cozumel
C-53 Wreck
33
Bahía Chankanaab
Skyreef 11
Costera Sur
Pueblo de Maíz 13
Carretera Transversal
San Gervasio 7
Hacienda Antigua 15
14 Mayan Bee Sanctuary
Playa Xhanan
Playa Bonita
Playa Los Cocos
Playa Santa Cecilia

Isla Cozumel

CARIBBEAN SEA

Paradise Beach 10
40
Mr Sancho's 8
Santa Rosa Wall
29
El Cedral Pass
16 El Cedral
Playa Palancar
Palancar Shallows
Palancar Caves
Parque Nacional Arrecifes de Cozumel
El Cielo
Laguna Colombia
Colombia Gardens
Chun Chacab
Devil's Throat
2 Punta Sur Eco Beach Park
Playa Encantada
28
Playa El Mirador
3 Playa Bonita
Playa de San Martín
4 Playa Chen Rio
31
30
5 Playa Punta Morena

Museo de Cozumel 1
27
18
Cozumel Snorkel Center
19
21
Passenger Ferry Dock (Muelle Fiscal)
CARIBBEAN SEA
32
17
35
38
37
39
26
Aldora Divers
22
Cozumel International Hospital
24
Deep Blue
34
20
12
Mercado Municipal
SAN MIGUEL DE COZUMEL

Av Rafael Melgar
Av 5 Norte
Av 10 Norte
Av 15 Norte
Av 20 Norte
Av 25 Norte
Av 30 Norte
C 10 Norte
C 8 Norte
C 6 Norte
C 4 Norte
C 2 Norte
Av Benito Juárez
C 1 Sur
C 3 Sur
C 5 Sur
C 7 Sur
Av 5 Sur
Av 10 Sur
Av 15 Sur
Av 20 Sur
Av 25 Sur
Av 30 Sur
Dr Adolfo Rosado Salas

0 — 200 m
0 — 0.1 miles

A B C D E F
5 6 7 8

For more see

- Top Experiences p126
- Experiences p132
- Eating p136
- Drinking p137
- Shopping p137

★ TOP EXPERIENCE

Diving & Snorkeling Isla Cozumel

A visit to Cozumel wouldn't be complete without exploring those world-famous reefs. Diving buffs will want to devote several days to these otherworldly sites, which have fantastic year-round visibility and an impressive variety of marine life, including rays, eels, groupers, barracudas, turtles, sharks and huge sponges.

PLANNING TIP
Evaluate conditions and plan your route carefully, selecting an exit point down-current beforehand, then staying alert for shifts in currents. Keep an eye out (and your ears open) for boat traffic.

Scan this QR code for info on diving sites and PADI-certified operators.

Dive at World-Class Sites

With more than 60 surrounding reefs, excellent visibility and an abundance of marine life, it's no wonder the late, great oceanographer Jacques Cousteau called Cozumel one of the world's top diving destinations. Among the island's many great sites, you'll find everything from challenging wall dives to shallow snorkeling spots.

One of the most famous dive sites, the **Santa Rosa Wall** is so large most people can see only a third of it on one tank. Regardless of where you're dropped, expect to find enormous overhangs and tunnels covered with corals and sponges. Stoplight parrotfish, black grouper and barracuda hang out here. The average visibility is 30m and the minimum depth is 10m, with an average closer to 25m. Carry a flashlight with you, even if you're diving at noon, as it will help to bring out the color of the coral at depth and illuminate the critters hiding in crevices.

El Cedral Pass is a shallow drift dive over a vibrant reef teeming with marine life, including splendid toadfish, which are endemic to Cozumel. Cave lovers should book a dive to **Palancar Caves** (pictured), with fascinating subterranean caverns and canyons to explore, as well as sandy areas and

PETER SZEKELY/ALAMY STOCK PHOTO

a drop-off into the deep blue. Located in Punta Sur Reef, the **Devil's Throat** is a cavern (for advanced divers only) that opens into a cathedral room with four tunnels, all of which make for some pretty hairy exploration. Butterflyfish, angelfish and whip corals abound at the reef.

There's also a wreck around a **C-53**, a WWII minesweeper sunk in 1999 to create an artificial reef at 24m. Divers can swim through its decks, hulls and corridors.

There are scores of dive operators on the island, including **ScubaTony** *(scubatony.com)*, **Aldora Divers** *(aldora.com)* and **Miri Adventures** *(instagram.com/miri_adventures)*. A half-day of diving (two tanks) on a boating excursion costs anywhere from US$120 to US$170. Intro dives, multiple-dive packages and PADI open-water certification are widely available.

QUICK BREAK
A short walk from Aqua Safari Pier (departure point for many dive operators), the Lobster Shack serves up the delicious crustacean as a roll, burrito or bowl.

Snorkel the Colorful Reefs

Just off Cozumel's coast, the ocean is warm, clear and full of stunning coral formations and majestic sea creatures. There are sites for every level of snorkeler, from the translucent sea-star bath at **El Cielo** to the **Colombia Gardens** with its massive, sponge-covered coral buttresses that can be seen from above, along with the occasional turtle or barracuda. Another prime spot is the **Palancar Shallows** (pictured), which has stunning underwater gardens with coral, sponges, fish, turtles, rays and eels. Around the island, there are numerous points of entry and countless tour operators to guide you deeper into the sea.

Lots of visitors rent snorkel gear and putter around the accessible sites just off the island and

KAROL KOZLOWSKI PREMIUM RM COLLECTION/ ALAMY STOCK PHOTO

in front of the beach clubs. The best clubs for snorkeling are **Buccanos** (p136), **Skyreef** (p134) and **Playa Palancar**. Of course, the best snorkel spots require getting into deeper water. Tour operators such as **Cozumel Snorkel Center** *(cozumelsnorkelcenter.com)* offer frequent trips to lively snorkel spots on the island's south, including Palancar, Colombia Gardens and El Cielo. Trips start at around M$1000 and often include sodas and snacks (and occasionally beer or margaritas).

Although it's a bit pricier *(from M$1500, plus M$140 park fee)*, you can also go out on a dive boat with operators such as **Deep Blue** *(deepblue cozumel.com)* to excellent snorkeling sites that include Palancar, Colombia Gardens, Cardona, San Clemente and Paradise, all near the island's southern end.

Experience Nightlife... Beneath the Sea

For those willing to brave the water after dark, night snorkeling is an exceedingly rewarding endeavor, as a whole different bunch of sea creatures (including small stingrays, octopus and squid) can be spotted and the vibe is delightfully spooky. Operators such as the recommended Night Snorkel Cozumel *(nightsnorkelcozumel.com; US$65)* provide all the gear you'll need, including wetsuit, mask, fins, snorkel and an extra-bright underwater flashlight for the surreal one-hour experience. They depart from the **Money Bar** (p137).

For divers, there are some even more exciting nocturnal options. Nearly all dive shops offer night dives in the marine park, while more experienced divers can join an otherworldly excursion offered by **Blackwater Cozumel** *(blackwatercozumel.com)*, where you'll dive in utter blackness (apart from the provided light sources) some 3km offshore. You'll feel like you're floating in outer space, and the creatures that drift by are decidedly alien.

MARACAIBO

One of Cozumel's least visited sites, Maracaibo is the island's southernmost reef, known as a spectacular yet challenging wall dive. It's for experienced divers only – you'll be plunging to depths of 40m in waters with strong currents. Common sightings include turtles, spotted eagle rays, nurse sharks and blacktip reef sharks.

Walk Isla Cozumel

San Miguel de Cozumel is a rewarding place to explore. On a stroll through the island's only sizable town (best done in the cooler late afternoon), you'll see a local side of life, with shops full of colorful handicrafts, fine views across the waterfront and public art that helps shed light on the region's complicated past.

START	END	LENGTH
Parque Benito Juarez	Plaza de las Dos Culturas	1.7km; 1¼ hours

1 Vibrant Hub of the Island

The heart of San Miguel de Cozumel is **Parque Benito Juarez**, set with palm trees and a photogenic clock tower, just a short stroll from the ferry terminal. Visitors come to take photos by the giant 'Cozumel' letters, browse food stands and survey the souvenir shops fringing the park.

2 Shops & Cafes

Like Playa del Carmen, San Miguel de Cozumel has its own Quinta Av (5th Ave). Here, it's a much more low-key affair, with a handful of shops, bars and eateries and it's never all that crowded. Stop for a pick-me-up at **COZ Coffee Roasting Company**.

3 Sculptural Reef

Turn left onto Calle 2 and head up to Av Melgar. Sculptures dot the waterfront, both north and south of the nearby ferry terminal. One of the most striking is the **Coral Reefs Monument**, an arclike sculpture adorned with fish, rays, sea turtles and two scuba divers. It was designed by the Mexican artist Rosa María Ponzanelli Quintero.

4 Art from the Sea

Heading right up Av Melgar, you'll pass more public artwork over the next few blocks, including the whimsical **Children and the Turtle** sculpture by Carlos Terrés. Another block on, turn your eyes seaward for a look at the **Barco Hundido**, an old capsized boat that's now covered in vibrant marine-themed murals.

5 Mexican Crafts

Cross the road at Calle 8 for a look inside **Los Cinco Soles**. This huge multiroom gallery features Cozumel's best collection of ceramics, carvings, tapestries and jewelry. All items are made in Mexico and showcase the craftsmanship of various regions, from the *alebrijes* (folk-art sculptures) of Oaxaca to Talavera pottery from Puebla and Tlaxcala.

6 The First Mestizo

Another three blocks to the north, check out the **Monumento al Mestizaje**, a large installation depicting the Spanish conquistador turned Maya advocate Gonzalo Guerrero with his wife Zacil-Ha and their child, allegedly the first *mestizo* (person of mixed indigenous and European ancestry) born in the Yucatán.

7 Clash of Cultures

From here, it's another 500m to the **Plaza de las Dos Culturas**, with statues of a Maya family and a Spanish missionary, set against a backdrop of a Maya pyramid. A good place to end your walk is at one of the nearby seaside restaurant-bars, such as **Hemingway**.

EXPERIENCES

Explore Cozumel's Past

MUSEUM

MAP: 1 P124 **E6**

For a primer on the entire island, set aside an hour or two to explore the sizable **Museo de Cozumel** *(M$136; Tue-Sun)*. The modern, thoughtfully designed museum is brimming with intrigue, starting with fossils and tiny wildlife scenes that shed light on the island's ecosystems – from wetlands to coastal dunes – while touching on unusual species such as the stingless bees.

Next, you'll enter the world of the ancient Maya. Highlights include a reconstruction of Cozumel's small Miramar Temple and the famous original column that supported the structure that depicts the goddess Ixchel in a position of giving birth. Another section touches on cosmology and spiritual beliefs with video projections.

The last part of the museum takes you from the time of the Spanish conquest to more recent times, with the swords of pirates on display, as well as large vats used for making chicle, a natural chewing gum that was a major Yucatán export in the 1920s.

Spend the Day at a Coastal Park

NATURE RESERVE

MAP: 2 P124 **B7**

The most rewarding stop, despite a steep entrance fee, is **Punta Sur Eco Beach Park** *(adult/child M$306/198)* at the island's southwestern tip. Ascend a winding staircase to the top of a lighthouse, tour a small nautical museum and visit a Maya ruin, all in the same vicinity near the park entrance. From here, head off on a short trail through coastal forest and mangroves to a small observation tower from where it's possible to spot migratory birds and crocodiles. Back in the car, continue along the unpaved coastal road, which is quite rutted and slow-going, to reach a white-sand beach with a shallow reef and a couple of open-air restaurants. There are also free boat tours *(noon, 1pm & 2pm)* around Laguna Colombia, where crocodiles are a guarantee and

ISLAND HISTORY

The Maya inhabited Cozumel from 300 CE, but after the Spaniards decimated their settlements, the island was deserted. In 1848 indigenous people fleeing the War of the Castes resettled Cozumel, and in the early 20th century, the population grew in step with the *chicle* trade. After the decline of this natural gum product, Cozumel's economy was kept afloat by a US airbase erected on the island during WWII. When the US military departed, Cozumel fell into a slump and people moved away. In the 1960s Cozumel gained fame for diving, and later as a cruise-ship destination.

flamingos are a possibility from November to March. You may also spot coatimundis, pygmy raccoons and tortoises.

Drive the Wild East Coast BEACHES

The eastern shore is the island's wildest part and presents some striking seascapes and many small blowholes. Swimming can be dangerous along most of the coast because of riptides and undertows, but the beaches are beautiful and perfect for strolling or enjoying the view while having a bite or a meal, though keep in mind sargassum seaweed may be present, especially from April through September.

Aptly named **Playa Bonita** (MAP: 3 P124 **C6**; Beautiful Beach) sits in a small bay and is a great spot to pull off and enjoy the scenery. Some 5.5km north, lovely **Playa Chen Rio** (MAP: 4 P124 **D5**) is one of the few spots where the water is sometimes calm enough for swimming, owing to a small rocky outcropping shielding the shore from waves. Another 3.5km north, photogenic **Playa Punta Morena** (MAP: 5 P124 **D5**) is a serene spot for a stroll. Chen Rio and Punta Morena have small, strategically placed bar-restaurants, and vendors also sell crafts.

Take a Surf Lesson SURFING

Several outfits in town offer surf lessons on the east coast, including the women-owned **Surf School by Highlife** (*surfcozumel.com; 90-minute lesson M$1600*), with instruction for all ages and ability levels (including first-timers). Transport to and from town is included, and multi-lesson package deals are available.

See the Reef by Submarine BOAT TRIP

MAP: 6 P124 **B3**

If you'd like to see what goes on beneath the sea, but aren't willing or able to scuba dive, there's **Atlantis Submarines** (*atlantissubmarines.mx; adult/child from US$99/55*). A trip down to the Chankanaab reef begins with a 10-minute boat ride out to the submarine, which you enter by walking backward through a hatch and down a ladder. The interior features large windows on either side, and as the captain lowers the sub down to the reef, coral, garden eels, lobsters and queen angel fish all come into view. The journey bottoms out at around 30m, and on its way up, the sub passes the C-53 shipwreck, which often has divers inside. The excursion lasts around two hours, with 45 minutes spent on the submarine.

Walk the Paths of the Ancients at San Gervasio ARCHAEOLOGICAL SITE

MAP: 7 P124 **D3**

For a deeper appreciation of island history, pay a visit to **San Gervasio** (*M$231; 8am-4pm*). The complex is thought to have

OTHER TOP BEACH CLUBS

Buccanos

MAP: 9 P124 **C2**

Just north of town, with decent snorkeling, a swimming pool, tiny beach and a recommended restaurant (minimum consumption M$400 per person).

Paradise Beach

MAP: 10 P124 **A5**

Kids love the floating water park and banana-boat rides. Adults love the massages, day beds and all-inclusive drinks *(adult/child US$68/45)*. Use of kayaks, SUP and snorkel gear costs extra *(US$14)*.

Skyreef

MAP: 11 P124 **B4**

There's no beach, but the snorkeling at this all-inclusive is superb, and there's plenty of good food and drink on hand (no admission, but typically asks a minimum spend of M$400).

contained the sanctuary of Ixchel, goddess of fertility, and is thus a site that Maya women – especially prospective mothers – traveled to for worship. While fascinating, don't expect Chichén Itzá–size temples. The structures are small and the clay idols of Ixchel were long ago destroyed by the Spaniards. Hiring a Sinaltur guide can help bring the place to life, with an hour or longer tour costing M$600. Go early in the day to beat the heat.

Fill a Day Full of Activities at Mr Sancho's

BEACH CLUB

MAP: 8 P124 **A5**

Cozumel has a wide variety of beach clubs. If you haven't been to one, here's how it works. You'll typically pay a set fee for admission and then will have access to lounge chairs, umbrellas, food, drink and a safely roped-off section of shoreline for swimming and snorkeling. **Mr Sancho's** *(mrsanchos.com; adult/child US$68/45)* is a favorite for its two pools (one with a swim-up bar), the use of kayaks and an all-you-can-eat and drink buffet. Optional add-ons include an aquatic park *(US$14)* with slides, trampolines and climbing surfaces out on the water. There's also horseback riding *(US$40)* and parasailing *(US$70)*.

Browse for Tropical Fruits

MARKET

MAP: 12 P124 **E8**

Locals after fresh produce and seafood head to the **Mercado Municipal** *(8am-3pm)*, an indoor marketplace that's packed with fruits and vegetables, freshly caught fish and carved meat. There are a few economical eateries, including surprises such as Loncheria Oasis, serving nasi goreng and other Indonesian fare. For more traditional bites, try Taqueria Molina, known for its egg breakfasts, tacos, tortas and juices.

Learn About the Maya — CULTURAL CENTER

MAP: 13 P124 C3

A short hop from San Gervasio (and 5km from San Miguel de Cozumel), the **Pueblo de Maíz** *(M$400)* is a thematic park that offers a kitschy but fun and interactive experience. Employees in elaborate Maya costumes paint your face with natural pigment, purify you with sacred incense and introduce you to a stone carving depicting the goddess Ixchel. A guide in a Maya headdress then escorts you into a series of *palapas* (thatched-roof structures), where hands-on activities highlight the ancient Maya lifestyle. You make tamales by hand, sample chocolate and *pozol* (a corn drink), and test the strength of agave fiber. The experience is mostly light-hearted, with lots of jokes about human sacrifice, but the drumming, dance and fire-stomping finale is intense and impressive.

Get Acquainted with Stingless Bees — ANIMAL SANCTUARY

MAP: 14 P124 D4

If you're thirsty for more curious connections to the Maya, drive five minutes down the road and check out the **Mayan Bee Sanctuary** *(adult/child M$152/114)*. The island was a major pre-Hispanic honey-producing center, and at this sanctuary guests meet stingless bees, taste their honey and visit a small cenote. The property features the impressive stone sculptures of artist Carlos Pacheco Polanco.

Taste Tantalizing Tequila — FARM

MAP: 15 P124 D4

If you can't swing a visit to Jalisco, stop by **Hacienda Antigua** *(free)*, a petite farm dedicated to Mexico's best-loved drink. Peruse displays about the tequila-making process, then taste samples from *blanco* to extra *añejo*. There's no pressure to buy, though most people do purchase a bottle or two.

Get Off the Beaten Track in El Cedral — VILLAGE

MAP: 16 P124 B5

A half-hour drive south of town, **El Cedral** is the oldest Maya settlement on the island. It costs M$60 to drive into the village, where a small Maya temple stands alongside a modern church, and a large adjacent plaza hosts markets and big events. Another attraction of El Cedral is the so-called **Jade Cavern** *(M$240)*, a bat-filled cenote that, for the Maya, was an entrance to the underworld. While not recommended for swimming, it's an atmospheric (but pricey) spot for photographs.

The best time to visit this small community is during the **Fiesta del Cedral**. Held in late April and early May, this annual celebration honors a group of War of the Castes refugees forced to flee the mainland and settle in Cozumel in 1848. The fair features rides, food stands, rodeos and traditional dance.

LISTINGS

Best Places for...

See p124 for map of locations

$ Budget $$ Midrange $$$ Top End

Eating

Cafes

COZ Coffee Roasting Company $
17 E7
One of the best little cafes on Quinta Av boasts a big menu of coffee, smoothies and frappes, plus breakfast fare, sandwiches and salads. *7am-9pm*

Maple Bakehouse $$
18 E6
An inviting spot for breakfast or a caffeinated recharge later in the day, with delicious baked goods, creative sandwiches and satisfying crepes. *7:30am-10pm*

Aquí + Ahora $$
19 E6
Charming spot for a bite or afternoon drinks, with an inviting ground-floor cafe and a rooftop terrace. Breakfast until noon. *8am-1am Tue-Sun*

Tacos & Burritos

Los Tacotales $
20 E8
Some of the best tacos on the island, along with flavor-packed burritos, tortas, quesadillas and rich *pozole* (a traditional soup). *noon-11pm*

Burritos Gorditos $
21 E6
Welcoming joint famous for vegetarian, chicken, pork and beef burritos, all *muy grande*! Come hungry. *8am-5pm Mon-Sat*

Date Night

Azul Madera $$$
22 D8
Inventive Mediterranean-inspired menu uses top-notch local ingredients, best enjoyed in the garden-fringed back patio. *5-10:30pm*

Casa Mission $$$
23 C3
Traditional Mexican and seafood restaurant with tableside Caesar salads, delicious king-crab legs and roving mariachis. *8am-11pm*

Kondesa $$$
24 D8
Upscale and innovative seafood restaurant in jungle-shrouded environs. Don't miss the lionfish cakes. *5-11pm*

Buccanos $$$
see  9 C2
This beach club goes upscale in the evenings with a cocktail lounge and fancy rooftop restaurant. *6-10:30pm Tue-Sat*

Seafood

Hemingway $$
25 C3
Atmospheric waterfront setting for sunset drinks and delicious grilled seafood. *9am-midnight*

Lobster Shack $$
26 D7
Casual, counter-service spot for lobster rolls, lobster burritos or lobster-topped bowls (of rice, beans, avocado and pico de gallo). *noon-9pm*

Guido's Restaurant $$$
 27 E6
Famed Italian spot with wood-fired pizzas, house-made pasta and some of

Cozumel's best seafood. Lovely courtyard. *2-10pm*

Dining on the Coast

Freedom in Paradise $$

 B6

The rasta-themed beach bar whips up plump coconut shrimp to go with tropical cocktails and lovely views. *10:30am-5pm*

Alberto's Beach Restaurant $$$

 A5

Laid-back spot for excellent seafood and a festive crowd. *9am-11pm*

Coconuts $$$

30 D5

Classic seafood (fish tacos, shrimp fajitas) in a colorful cliff-top setting above a rocky stretch of shoreline. *10am-7pm*

El Pescador $$$

 D5

Dig your feet in the sand while enjoying ceviches, nachos and margaritas at this prime spot between two beaches. *10am-5pm*

Drinking

Live Music

Wet Wendy's

32 E7

One of several buzzing bars on Quinta Av, drawing an easy-going crowd who come for the huge frozen margaritas and live music. *11am-midnight*

Money Bar

 B4

This beach club, 7km south of town, is an enticing spot for happy hour, with live music and fiery sunset views. *8am-10pm*

Beer & Cocktails

Cervecería Punta Sur

 E8

The island's first and only microbrewery serves tasty local brews and a mean lionfish pizza. *noon-11pm*

Woody's

 E7

Prime location just off the main plaza for people-watching, cold drinks and barbecue, plus sports on TV and live music. *10am-11:30pm*

La Monina

 B3

This eatery and bar has a beautiful sunset location. It's great in the daytime too, with two-for-one cocktails and you can snorkel and swim just off the beach. *8am-11pm*

Shopping

Handicrafts & Jewelry

Parque Benito Juarez

 E7

On weekend evenings, craft sellers ply their wares in the park – handmade jewelry, bags, clothing and various food vendors. *5-11pm Fri-Sun*

Sergio's

 E7

Beautifully made jewellery featuring unique stones and settings fashioned from silver from Taxco, Mexico's silver-mining capital. *11am-7pm Mon-Sat*

Art

Galeria Azul

 F6

Just off the beaten path, this gallery features the Caribbean-inspired work of glass artist Greg Dietrich. *11am-7pm Mon-Fri*

Chocolate

Mayan Cacao Company

40 A5

At Playa Mia Beach Club (16km south of town), this place has tastings, tours and workshops, plus decadent chocolate bars with unique ingredients (like chipotle chili). *9am-4pm*

★ WORTH A TRIP

Puerto Morelos

Stretching along a picturesque beach just south of Cancún, Puerto Morelos is one of the Riviera Maya's most laid-back towns. There's fine snorkeling on the barrier reef offshore, and you can learn about native plants and see wildlife at a nature reserve just outside of town.

PLANNING TIP
Colectivos from Cancún or Playa del Carmen will drop you at the highway turnoff to Puerto Morelos. From there it's a 2.5km walk into town, or take a taxi or town-bound *colectivo (M$10)*.

Snorkeling the Reef

Brilliantly contrasted stripes of bright green and dark blue separate the shore from the barrier reef – a tantalizing sight for divers and snorkelers. Various operators around town run tours, though you can also head to the pier, just off the main plaza, where a boat cooperative runs tours *(per person M$450)* continuously through the day. On a standard two-hour excursion, you'll head to a prime reef spot (usually five to 10 minutes away) to snorkel amid a kaleidoscope of aquatic species. You might spot sea turtles, nurse sharks, stingrays, moray eels, lobsters and loads of colorful tropical fish. You'll have about 45 minutes there before moving to a second spot for more reef immersion.

Nature Encounters

A short taxi ride *(M$150)* south of Puerto Morelos is a lush remnant of the once-vast coastal forests covering the northern Yucatán Peninsula. Despite the name, the 65-hectare **Jardín Botánico Dr Alfredo Barrera Marín** *(adult/child M$120/50, 8am-4pm, weekdays only)* feels less like a manicured botanical garden and more like an untamed nature reserve, and the wildlife (including spider monkeys; pictured) is as much a draw as the diverse plant species (pictured).

SHIRLEY KILPATRICK/ALAMY STOCK PHOTO

When you arrive, pay your admission and borrow a map (or photograph the sign). While fairly easy to follow, the 2km trail that loops around the property has a few notable detours. Walking counterclockwise, you'll pass through sections devoted to epiphytes, palms and ferns. You'll also see some 15th-century ruins, a re-created encampment of *chicle* (gum) harvesters, a wetland of mangroves and a three-story lookout tower you can climb.

QUICK BREAK

El Nicho is the best place in town for breakfast, coffee and sandwiches. **El Pesquero** is a favorite for uncomplicated seafood in a rustic setting with sand floors and a thatched roof.

Evening Handicraft Market

At night, the main plaza in town, **Parque Fundadores** *(5-10pm Wed-Sun)*, springs to life as a handicraft market, where vendors sell their handmade ceramics, jewelry, paintings, textiles and more.

Cancún & the Riviera Maya Toolkit

Parque del Jaguar (p106), Tulum
JESS KRAFT/SHUTTERSTOCK

Family Travel

Few places offer more to see and do for youngsters than the Yucatán, with its mix of beaches, boat trips and snorkeling adventures, plus opportunities to clamber around ancient ruins and even see monkeys in the treetops.

Getting Around

If you're renting a car, you may want to bring your own car seat, as agencies often add US$7 or more per day to the cost of the car. Buses have comfortable seats, usually with onboard movies, and most have bathrooms. *Colectivos* (shared vans) can be less comfortable, but at least the rides aren't typically very long.

DISCOUNTS

Museums, archeological sites, water parks and even some hotels offer discounts for children. You'll also find family-ticket deals at some child-friendly attractions. When purchasing bus or train tickets, look for half-price deals for kids aged five to 12.

Accommodations

Family rooms are widely available, and many hotels will put an extra bed in a room at little extra cost. You can find rooms with air-conditioning nearly everywhere and wi-fi is standard. Plenty of places have pools and some have beach clubs. You'll also find child-friendly channels on the TV and/or access to streaming services like Netflix – ideal when your kids need some downtime.

Essential Supplies

All *farmacias* (pharmacies) have diapers, painkillers, cortisone creams and nonsteroidal anti-inflammatory drugs (NSAIDs). Less easily found are high-quality sunscreens; bring these from home.

Diaper Emergencies

Facilities for changing diapers can be found in some shopping centers and restaurants.

Dining Out

You have a better chance of finding child-friendly menus closer to the tourist centers. If your kid is a finicky eater, consider packing a lunch when visiting small towns, where menu options may be more limited.

ARKADIJ SCHELL/SHUTTERSTOCK

Accommodations

There's plenty of variety for all budget levels in Cancún and the Riviera Maya, from festive hostels to luxe beachfront hotels.

Where to Stay if You Love...

Blissing Out on the Beach

Cancún's Zona Hotelera (p47) The resort-studded coastline has beautiful white-sand beaches – the perfect backdrop to long walks, bike rides and alfresco meals.

Local Culture

Cancún Centro (p31) Staying in Cancún's more affordable downtown puts you near family-friendly parks, food vendors, lively markets and street art, and the beach is an easy bus ride away.

We love to stay on...

Isla Holbox (p75). It's easy to fall under the spell of this enchanting, artfully rustic island. Sure, you'll have to take a longish bus ride and ferry to get there, but it's well worth the effort to unwind in a remote getaway, whether overnighting in a beachfront oasis or an eco-hotel made of traditional materials.

HOW MUCH FOR A NIGHT IN

Hostel dorm bed
M$500

Guesthouse
M$1000–1600

Beachfront hotel
M$2500–5000

Dining & Nightlife

Playa del Carmen (p87) Stay within strolling distance of Quinta Avenida, the city's electrifying heart, with its open-sided restaurants, music-filled bars and nightclubs.

Outdoor Adventures

Tulum (p103) Head out on a wide range of day trips, from cycling around the ruins of Cobá to boating and wildlife encounters in Sian Ka'an Biosphere Reserve.

Diving & Snorkeling

Cozumel (p123) Fringed by colorful coral reefs full of marine life, Cozumel is the gateway to some of Mexico's most impressive dive sites, plus snorkeling off the beach.

Food, Drink & Nightlife

Allergies & Intolerances

People with food allergies and intolerances will have to take extra care when eating out. Sometimes seemingly vegetarian dishes may contain lard or chicken stock. With corn being the staple ingredient, many dishes are naturally gluten free.

HOW TO SAY

I'm allergic to... *Soy alérgico...*
Nuts *a las nueces*
Seafood *a los mariscos*
Dairy products *a los productos lácteos*
Gluten *al gluten*

HOW TO ASK...

Is there a vegetarian/vegan option?
¿Hay una opción vegetariana/vegana?
Is this gluten-free?
¿Esto es libre de gluten?
Does this contain nuts?
¿Esto contiene nueces?

BREAKFAST OF CHAMPIONS

Eggs are essential building blocks of the morning meal and can be served a number of different ways, usually accompanied by tortillas, refried beans and fruit. You should also try *chilaquiles*: strips of fried corn tortillas topped with salsa, cheese and other goodness.

Yucatecan Dishes

The Yucatán has some unique dishes you won't find elsewhere. A few favorites: *salbutes* (fried tortillas topped with shredded turkey or chicken), *panuchos* (like *salbutes*, but with a layer of beans) and *papadzules* (diced hard-boiled eggs wrapped in corn tortillas and topped with pumpkin seeds and tomato sauce).

HOW TO... Pay the Bill

Generally, you won't be presented with the bill until you ask for it. Attract your server's attention by saying *'disculpe'* or *'perdón'* (excuse me), *'la cuenta, por favor'* (the bill, please).

Splitting the bill If you want to split the bill, say *'¿Podemos dividir la cuenta, por favor?'* (Can we divide the bill, please?)

Tipping At some touristy places, the tip may already be included. Find out by asking *'¿La propina está incluída?'* (Is the tip included?) In restaurants, 10% to 15% is standard. If you're paying with a credit card, the server will bring the card reader to your table and may ask if you want to add the tip directly to the total.

PRICE RANGES

The following price ranges refer to the average cost of a main course.

$ less than M$100

$$ M$100–200

$$$ more than M$200

OPENING HOURS

Cafes 7:30am to 5pm; some stay open as late as 9pm

Restaurants noon to 10pm; many open as early as 8am

Bars 4pm to 2am weekdays, with earlier opening times on weekends

Going Out

Sunset Drinks A proper night out in the Yucatán often begins with cocktails by the seaside. The margarita is a fine drink of choice for a sundowner, though you can also opt for a *mez-calito* (made with mezcal rather than tequila) or a mojito (made with rum and mint).

Bar Hopping After grabbing a bite to eat, it's time to hit the nightlife. In Playa del Carmen that means trolling the bars along Quinta Avenida, while in Cancún the action is split between the raucous nightclubs of the Zona Hotelera and more laid-back drinking spots in Centro.

Clubs If it's dancing you're after, keep in mind that most of the clubs are fairly empty before 11pm. Prime time for dancing and people-watching is around midnight.

Dress Code Most clubs are pretty casual when it comes to dress, with 'smart casual' being the general rule.

HOW MUCH FOR A

Street taco
M$30–40

Bag of churros
M$50

Meal in a market
M$130

Breakfast plate at a midrange restaurant
M$100–160

Dinner for two at an upscale restaurant
M$1400–2200

Cappuccino
M$50–80

Beer
M$50–90

Margarita
M$120–200

SEREGAM/SHUTTERSTOCK

LGBTIQ+ Travelers

Cancún and the Riviera Maya are fairly broad-minded about sexuality. LGBTIQ+ travelers rarely attract open discrimination.

Pride Fests & Other Big Fests

June is the month for catching two big Pride events on the Caribbean coast: Playa Pride (in Playa del Carmen) and Cancún Pride. These feature colorful costumes, beautifully attired drag queens, rainbow-painted cars and floats and abundant joie de vivre, plus plenty of music-filled parties before and after. Exact dates change annually, so check in January for the schedule.

If you're here earlier in the year, try to catch **Arena Festival** *(arena.mx)*, the biggest LGBTIQ+ dance-music fest in Mexico. It takes place over six days in late January or early February in Playa del Carmen. In early April, Isla Mujeres hosts **Utopia** *(utopiaisla.com)*, a brilliant LGBTIQ+ festival featuring top DJs spinning over four nights of revelry in an enchanting island setting.

Best Gay Beaches

In **Cancún**, Playa Defines and Playa Gaviota Azul draw a wide cross-section of visitors, including the LGBTIQ+ crowd. In **Playa del Carmen**, there's another unofficial gay gathering spot near the Mamitas Beach. It's directly in front of and just north of the Mamitas Beach Club.

GAYTOWN, MEXICO

In general, the most gay-friendly destinations are Cancún, Playa del Carmen and Tulum. Check gaymexicomap.com for LGBTIQ+ lodging, tours and nightlife.

NEW AFRICA/SHUTTERSTOCK

LGBTIQ+ TOURS

In Playa del Carmen, Pink Flamingo Gay Tours *(pinkflamingogay.tours)* focuses on visits to Maya ruins and adventure travel, including excursions into the Sian Ka'an Biosphere Reserve.

Big Nights Out

Cancún is the epicenter of the LGBTIQ+ party scene, with some outstanding clubs. In addition to gay-friendly spots like Coco Bongo (p55), you'll find major hotspots like 11:11 (p43) and Laser Hot Bar Beer & Queer (p43). In Playa del Carmen, the place to be is Club Provenza (with go-go dancers) and Sirenas (with fun drag shows).

Health & Safe Travel

Travelers to Cancún and the Riviera Maya need to be mindful about food, water and those intense tropical rays.

THEFT

Pickpocketing and bag-snatching are relatively minor risks, but it's wise to stay alert on buses and in crowded bus terminals and airports. Don't leave valuables unattended while you swim, and don't leave anything valuable-looking in a parked vehicle. Muggings are rare, but to avoid injury don't resist.

Sunburn & Heat Dangers

To protect yourself from excessive sun exposure, stay out of the midday sun, wear sunglasses and a wide-brimmed hat, and apply sunscreen with SPF 30 or higher, providing both UVA and UVB protection. A long-sleeved rash shirt is an essential investment here. Many cenotes and some marine sanctuaries don't allow sunscreen (regardless of any ecofriendly labeling) since it pollutes the water. Drink plenty of fluids (not alcohol, which is dehydrating) and avoid strenuous exercise when the temperature is high.

Tap Water

Tap water isn't safe to drink. Most portable water filters don't provide protection against viruses.

QUICK INFO

Swim Safety

Avoid swimming if there's a red flag. At other times, swim near lifeguards if possible.

Privacy

Ask permission before photographing someone.

Marijuana

Best avoided. Possession is decriminalized, but police arrest users to extract bribes.

Insurance

A travel insurance policy to cover theft, loss and medical problems is a good idea. Some policies specifically exclude riskier activities such as scuba diving and motorcycling. Some US health-insurance policies stay in effect (at least for a limited time) if you travel abroad, but it's worth checking exactly what you'll be covered for in Mexico.

MOSQUITOES

Mosquito-borne infections are a risk – Zika and dengue being the most high profile. In buggy areas, wear insect repellent.

Responsible Travel

Follow these tips to leave a lighter footprint, support local and have a positive impact on communities.

Public Transport over Car Rentals

First-time visitors often wonder how easy it is to get around without a car rental. It's quite doable and, in fact, it adds to the travel experience, allowing you to meet locals along the way. Buses and trains are quite comfy and allow you to focus on the scenery rather than the road. *Colectivos* are less comfy but great for zipping between towns along the coast.

Ecofriendly Dining

There's a lot of greenwashing going on, but you can still find restaurants deeply committed to sustainability, including **Aldea Kuká** (p85) on Holbox and **Hartwood** (p118; pictured) in Tulum.

FROM LEFT: PHORTUN/SHUTTERSTOCK; NICHOLAS GILL/ALAMY STOCK PHOTO

OUR PICK

Jungle Adventures

Learn about the forest and wildlife on a tour led by the local Maya community, descendants of former *chicleros* (natural gum harvesters) in **Punta Laguna** (p116).

Slow Travel

Skip the ATVs and jet skis and focus on low-impact tourism, which is better for the environment and offers deeper connections to the natural world. Look for walking, cycling, sailing or kayaking excursions. The Zona Hotelera's west shore abuts Laguna Nichupté, which makes a memorable setting for paddling adventures, like those offered by **Go Kayak Cancún** (p53).

Resources

- **theyucatantimes.com** Insight into local, sustainable travel across the peninsula.
- **ceakumal.org** Nonprofit devoted to sustainability; accepts volunteers for turtle monitoring and reef restoration.

ANCESTRAL BEEKEEPING

The small stingless honey bee has long been revered by the Maya. Known locally as *xunan kab*, the endangered bee produces a unique honey used in holistic medicine, with products available at some markets.

Get on Your Bike

Bicycles are a handy way to get around while lowering your carbon footprint. Cancún's Zona Hotelera has the excellent **Ciclopista** (p53), which runs for 13km between Coral Beach in the north to Punta Nizac in the south. Playa del Carmen's Quinta Avenida is a handy vehicle-free thoroughfare for reaching the beaches north of the center, while Tulum has several key bike paths from the town center: one out to Parque del Jaguar and another down to the beach. Isla Mujeres and Holbox are also good for navigating by pedal power.

ARTISAN RESPECT

Haggling with artisans over handicrafts is discouraged as it can be disrespectful and doesn't take into account the cost of raw materials or the many days or weeks of hard work. Many artisans support their families with their sales.

Climate Change & Travel

It's impossible to ignore the impact we have when traveling; Lonely Planet urges all travelers to engage with their travel carbon footprint, which will mainly come from air travel. While there often isn't an alternative, travelers can look to minimize the number of flights they take, opt for newer aircrafts and use cleaner ground transport, such as trains. One proposed solution – purchasing carbon offsets – unfortunately does not cancel out the impact of individual flights. While most destinations will depend on air travel for the foreseeable future, for now, pursuing ground-based travel where possible is the best course of action.

The **UN Carbon Offset Calculator** shows how flying impacts a household's emissions.

offset calculator

The **ICAO's carbon emissions calculator** allows visitors to analyse the CO_2 generated by point-to-point journeys.

icao.int

Accessible Travel

Maya Ruins

Once past the steep entrance ramps into Tulum, the majority of the ruins are accessible along unpaved paths. Chichén Itzá has ramped entrances and flat unpaved paths crisscrossing the entire site. The **Gran Museo de Chichén Itzá** (p60), which opened in 2024, is also accessible, though it's a 2.5km drive from the ruins.

Quinta Avenida

Playa del Carmen's vibrant pedestrian strip is completely accessible. The long car-free promenade is lined with accessible shops, restaurants, bars and cafes, and there's also the **Parque los Fundadores** (p94), where you can take in performances and street food.

ACCOMMODATIONS

Newer hotels and resorts have accessible rooms, with the best options along the Caribbean coast. Cancún leads the pack: some resorts offer wheelchair-accessible rooms, roll-in showers, pools with step-free areas and direct beach access.

Cozumel

This island is a decent choice for a vacation, with its smooth, cobblestone-free paths, an array of accessible shops, restaurants and beach clubs. The ferries there are also accessible.

A handful of beaches have accessible parking and ramps down to the shore. Cancún's most accessible beach is **Playa Las Perlas**, where visitors can borrow amphibious wheelchairs or adapted lounge chairs, and there's a smooth mat leading into the water. Playa del Carmen has a lovely accessible beach, **Punta Esmeralda** (p94), which also has specialized equipment (free to borrow) and shaded *palapas* (thatched-roof huts). Both beaches have staff on hand to provide assistance from 9am to 5pm.

TRAIN TRAVEL

The new Tren Maya has fully accessible trains and stations. On the downside, once you arrive, you'll still need to take an onward bus or taxi since the stations are far from city centers.

Resources

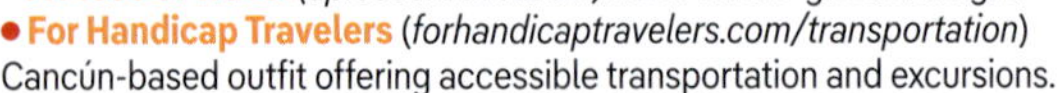

- **A Piece of Travel** (*apieceoftravel.com*) Keen on-the-ground insight.
- **For Handicap Travelers** (*forhandicaptravelers.com/transportation*) Cancún-based outfit offering accessible transportation and excursions.

apieceoftravel.com

Nuts & Bolts

Opening Hours

Places on Sunday can be a ghost town. Except for chain stores, many businesses and restaurants are closed.

Archaeological sites 8am to 4pm

Government offices & services 9am to 5pm Monday to Friday, sometimes 10am to 3pm Saturday

Shops 10am to 6pm

Restaurants Lunch noon to 4pm, dinner 6pm to 9pm

Banks 9am to 5pm Monday to Friday

Cafes 8am to 9pm

Cenotes 9am to 5pm

Museums 9am to 5pm Tuesday–Sunday

QUICK INFO

Time zone Hora del Centro (GMT/UTC–6)

Area code 55

Emergency number 911

Population 1.9 million

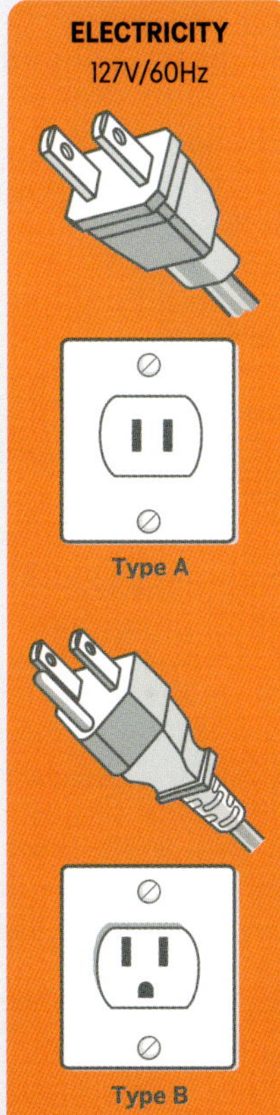

Toilets & Other Essentials

Toilets Public toilets are rare. Use hotels, restaurants, museums or bus terminals (typically M$10).

Smoking Banned in public indoor spaces.

Weights & Measures Mexico uses the metric system.

Public Holidays

Año Nuevo (New Year's Day) January 1

Día de la Constitución (Constitution Day) February 5

Día del Nacimiento de Benito Juárez (Anniversary of Benito Juárez' birth) March 21

Día del Trabajo (Labor Day) May 1

Día de la Independencia (Independence Day) September 16

Día de la Revolución (Revolution Day) November 20

Día de Navidad (Christmas Day) December 25

In addition, some places close on the following optional holidays.

Día de la Bandera (National Flag Day) February 24

Viernes Santo (Good Friday) Two days before Easter

Día de la Raza (Columbus' 'discovery' of the New World) October 12

Día de Muertos (Day of the Dead) November 1 and 2

Language

Basics

Hello.
Hola. *o·la*

Goodbye.
Adiós. *a·dyos*

Yes.
Sí. *see*

No.
No. *no*

Thank you.
Gracias. *gra·syas*

Excuse me.
Perdón. *per·don*

Sorry.
Lo siento. *lo syen·to*

Please.
Por favor. *por fa·vor*

You're welcome.
De nada. *de na·da*

Fast Phrases

Do you speak English?
¿Habla inglés? *a·bla een·gles (pol)*

I don't understand.
Yo no entiendo. *yo no en·tyen·do*

I'd like...	**Quisiera...** *kee·sye·ra*
a beer.	**una cerveza.** *oo·na ser·ve·sa*
a coffee.	**un café.** *oon ka·fe*
a white wine.	**un vino blanco.** *oon vee·no blan·ko*
a red wine.	**un vino tinto.** *oon vee·no teen·to*

The bill, please.
La cuenta, por favor. *la kwen·ta por fa·vor*

How much is this?
¿Cuánto cuesta esto? *kwan·to kwes·ta es·to*

Where are the toilets?
¿Dónde están los baños? *don·de es·tan los ba·nyos*

Could you please speak more slowly?
¿Puede hablar más despacio, por favor?
pwe·de a·blar mas des·pa·syo por fa·vor

Where's the nearest ATM?
¿Dónde está el cajero automático más cercano?
don·de es·ta el ka·khe·ro ow·to·ma·tee·ko mas ser·ka·no

Can I have a receipt, please?
¿Podría darme un recibo, por favor?
po·dree·a dar·me oon re·see·bo por fa·vor

Numbers

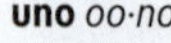
uno *oo·no*

dos *dos*

tres *tres*

cuatro *kwa·tro*

cinco *seen·ko*

Good to know

Mexican Spanish pronunciation is easy, as most sounds have equivalents in English. Note that **kh** is a throaty sound (like the 'ch' in the Scottish loch), **v** and **b** are both pronounced like a soft English 'v' (between a 'v' and a 'b'), and **r** is strongly rolled.

Keep in mind that in some parts of Mexico the letters **ll** and y are pronounced like the 'll' in 'million', but in most areas they are pronounced like the 'y' in 'yes,' and this is how they are represented in our pronunciation guides.

Spanish has a formal and informal word for 'you' (**usted** and **tú** respectively).

FALSE FRIENDS

Some Spanish words look like English words but have a different meaning! The word **sopa** sounds like soap but actually means soup. Soap is **jabón**. Likewise **éxito** means success while exit is **salida**. **Sensible** in Spanish means sensitive and **nudo** is knot.

Signs

Salida Exit
Entrada Entrance
Abierto Open
Cerrado Closed
Hombres/Varones Men
Mujeres/Damas Women
Servicios/Baños Toilets
Estación de tren Train station
Aeropuerto Airport
Calle Street
Prohibido Prohibited
No fumadores Nonsmoking

Listen for

Your passport, please.
Su pasaporte, por favor. *soo pa·sa·por·te por fa·vor*
Are you travelling on your own?
¿Está viajando solo/a? *es·ta vya·khan·do so·lo/a*

SOME MEXICAN SLANG TO LEARN

Scatter some of these slang expressions into your conversations.

¿Qué onda? What's up?/What's going on?
¡Qué padre! How cool!
Fregón. Really good/cool/awesome.
Irse de reventón. Go partying.
¡Vámonos de reventón! Let's go party!
Me late. Sounds really good to me.

seis *seys*

siete *sye·te*

ocho *o·cho*

nueve *nwe·ve*

diez *dyes*

Index

Sights p000 Map pages p000

See also separate subindexes for:
Eating p156
Drinking p157
Shopping p157

Eating

Drinking

Shopping

Send Us Your Feedback

We love to hear from travelers – your comments help make our books better. We read every word, and we guarantee that your feedback goes straight to the authors. Visit lonelyplanet.com/contact to submit your updates and suggestions.

Note: We may edit, reproduce and incorporate your comments in Lonely Planet products such as guidebooks, websites and digital products, so let us know if you are happy to have your name acknowledged. For a copy of our privacy policy visit lonelyplanet.com/legal.

Acknowledgements

Cover photograph: Cancún, Quintana Roo, Mexico. Gerard Puigmal/Getty Images ©

Back photograph: Cycling near the ancient ruins of Cobá. Dear Bunbuamas/Shutterstock

THIS BOOK

Destination Editor
Lauren Keith

Cartographer
Julie Sheridan

Production Editor
Martijn Vos

Image Editor
Fergal Condon

Cover Researcher
Daisy Korpics

Coordinating Editor
Andrew Bain

Assisting Cartographer
Dorothy Davidson

Thanks to
Ronan Abayawickrema, Melanie Dankel, Barbara Delissen, Alison Killilea, Kellie Langdon, Maura Murphy

Published by Lonely Planet Global Limited
CRN 554153
2nd edition – Oct 2025
ISBN 978 1 78868 429 3

10 9 8 7 6 5 4 3 2 1
Printed in China